Contents

Introduction

INTRODUCTION

Welcome to your Student Book on the AQA Short Story Anthology, *Telling Tales*, with stories by writers from the last hundred years of writing. We hope you enjoy these stories during your GCSE course and later in life.

Some of the stories deal with things that you may be familiar with, and may even be an expert on: family ties and conflicts, friendships, strong emotions and discoveries about yourself and other people. All the stories explore relationships and conflicts (*between* people and *within* people) similar to the poems in the AQA Anthology clusters on 'Love and relationships' or 'Power and conflict'. Some of the stories might make you think 'I've felt that' or 'I've thought that' – and others may make you think 'I wouldn't feel that' or 'I wouldn't think that'. Either way, the stories have the power to develop, challenge or even change the way you think and feel about yourself and about life.

Your Student Book will help you to make the most of these stories and of your GCSE. It will develop your skills in reading and responding, and help you to appreciate the writers' skills in sharing their insights and engaging you as their reader. It will also develop your skills in writing for your GCSE English Literature exam.

Here's how we have organised the book for you:

Exploring and writing about short stories

- Each unit leads you through a short story. It ensures you build a thorough understanding of the plot, the ideas and the methods that the writer has used to present situations, characters and ideas to readers.

- As well as focusing closely on the text, each unit provides activities for discussion and creative approaches to help you think further about the stories. On Cambridge Elevate you will find readings of the stories and video interviews with experts discussing key aspects of the stories. All these will develop your understanding, interpretation and analysis of the short stories.

- Your work with each story will result in notes and focused responses on aspects of the stories that are important for GCSE. These will also be useful when you write about two stories and revise for your exam.

Preparing for your examination

This part gives you practice and guidance to prepare for your examination. It also provides examples of answers, so you can use the skills you have developed and assess where your skills are strong and where to focus your effort to improve. In addition, it includes a table of themes and ideas in each of the stories, which will also be useful preparation for your exam.

We hope that you will enjoy using these resources, not only to support your GCSE study, but to see that this collection of short stories has plenty to say about life around you – and within you.

Peter Thomas, Series Editor

Introducing Telling Tales

MODERN SHORT STORIES AND GCSE ENGLISH LITERATURE

In the AQA Short Story Anthology – *Telling Tales* – there are seven modern short stories, dealing with aspects of love, loss, memory and discovery.

You will need to study them all so that you can answer a question on the one named in the exam, and another of your choice from the Anthology.

Modern short stories

What makes a short story different from a story told in a novel is – obviously – that it is short. Starting from this point, it's worth looking at what this means for the writer – and for the reader.

Firstly, the story told has to be completed in a few pages. This means no sub-plots, wide range of characters or development of a character or situation over a long time-span.

This lack of space to develop a character over the length of a novel may seem a disadvantage. However, a writer can show change within a character as a result of an experience. It is also possible to change a reader's response to a character or situation by manipulating the viewpoint or by keeping back some detail of information until later.

Secondly, the writer has to establish character and setting very quickly to allow the development of the short story.

This may also seem a disadvantage, because it means necessary information may be loaded into the opening paragraphs. However, this can be an advantage if a writer uses a few small details to trigger the reader's impressions.

Thirdly, the story has to keep the reader focused throughout in case they miss something. Unlike a novel, which might be read over several days or weeks, a short story is usually read in one burst. This makes it a more condensed text, and one needing closer reading.

Some short stories end by explaining what has been going on – possibly in a surprising way. Others end by leaving the reader asking questions – sometimes in a disturbing way. A successful ending leaves the reader wanting to know more – but having to read the story again to make sure they have not missed anything the first time.

Developing your response

Before you take your GCSE English Literature exam, you need to be sure that you understand what the stories are about. Then you need to be sure that you can explain your understanding based on details of characters and situations in the stories. Finally, you need to be able to show how the ideas in (and triggered by) the stories connect with other Anthology stories and with ideas about life as you and other readers may see it.

This guide will help you to identify the level you are working at, and what you need to do to improve.

LITERATURE SKILLS AND STUDY FOCUS AREAS

GCSE tests your understanding of:

- writers' ideas and purposes
- how these are conveyed by the writer's craft.

These are the two essential aspects of GCSE Literature study and response. You need to have something to say about both aspects in any story you write about.

Developing understanding of ideas and techniques

You can prepare for this by deciding what the main idea and the main technique in each story are. For example, you could work with any of the following – and add more of your own:

Writers' ideas in the short stories include the idea that:

- losing your means of living could result in a father persuading his own son to join the army to get compensation if he got killed (in 'Korea')
- people can conquer low self-esteem to form relationships despite differences in culture, nationality or status (in 'My Polish Teacher's Tie')

- older people can be driven to extremes by loneliness, jealousy or resentment (in 'Chemistry')
- someone can assert their own individuality by standing up against 'official' views about culture and history (in 'Invisible Mass of the Back Row').

Writers' techniques in the short stories include:

- using a local dialect to create a sense of place and community (in 'Odour of Chrysanthemums')
- using dialogue to suggest a character's attitude, for example the Head's 'Oh, er – Mrs, er – Carter' in 'My Polish Teacher's Tie' to show that he is not really sure who Carla is because she is 'only' a canteen assistant
- ending a story with the reader wondering whether a father has cooked a special supper for his children as a way of saving family honour through a death-sacrifice (in 'A Family Supper')
- using symbolic detail to provide contrast, for example Penelope Lively's description of Sandra's idealised view of her future life contrasted with the real world's ugliness and dirt in 'The Darkness Out There'.

The darkness was out there and it was a part of you and you would never be without it, ever.

(From 'The Darkness Out There' by Penelope Lively, Unit 7)

Here are examples of different levels of response to writers' ideas and purposes for two stories. You will explore more about the writers' craft as you work with each story.

You will see that the best responses link ideas and craft. Read them and think about how they show a move from 'basic' responses that are relevant and supported by quotation, to skills of understanding and interpretation that explain feelings, motives or reasons and develop ideas by relating them to broader ideas, perspectives and contexts.

'Invisible Mass of the Back Row'

It's about a girl who goes to school in Jamaica where she gets treated like she's not very bright and doesn't like it: 'my limbs shaking uncontrollably, sweat dripping from my armpits, my eyes inflamed. My belly aches. I am petrified.'

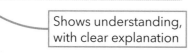

Shows a relevant response, supported with quotation

The story follows a Jamaican girl called Hortense who is glad to get away from her school in Jamaica to join her parents in England but she finds she is still treated as if she is not very bright because she was put in 'the hottest, baddest stream in the first year, only second to one six, the remedial stream'.

Shows understanding, with clear explanation

The story is about a Jamaican girl called Hortense who feels angry about the way she is punished at school for her rebellious opinion about Christopher Columbus. She is glad to leave the school and Jamaica to go to school in England where her parents live, but comes up against the English view of Columbus as a hero again. This time, however, she stands up for all her black friends on 'the back row' and feels that she has claimed 'a victory' by challenging the colonial view of history.

Shows exploration and evaluation

'The Darkness Out There'

It's about two teenagers who are in the school Good Neighbours' Club and do Saturday jobs for an old lady called Mrs Rutter whose husband got killed in the war. Sandra is a bit of a dreamer ('She would fall in love and she would get a good job') and Kerry is leaving school to work at the Blue Star garage.

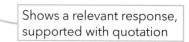

Shows a relevant response, supported with quotation

The story is about two teenagers meeting an old woman who seems kind and cosy until they find out she let a German pilot die because she hated Germans because they killed her husband. It's only later on you realise this side to her, because at first the writer describes her as 'a cottage-loaf of a woman' with a 'creamy smiling pool of a face'. The writer also makes you think that Kerry, the boy, is less bright than Sandra, the girl, but you realise at the end that he is more mature than she is because he understands Mrs Rutter better.

Shows understanding, with clear explanation

I think Penelope Lively uses the story to show how people are not the same as they appear at first. She does this by making the reader think that Mrs Rutter, the old lady, is a friendly, warm-hearted person, but there are hints that she may be different ('her eyes snapped and darted'), which makes her seem more dangerous. The other side of her is shown when Lively makes her tell them she left the German pilot to die in agony because she had lost her husband – 'Tit for tat'. Lively doesn't make her out to be cruel or evil – just someone whose own suffering made her do something that seems cruel. It makes the reader think that people aren't good and bad like black and white, but that there are 'dark' bits to anyone's nature, which is something that Sandra has to realise for the first time.

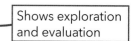

Shows exploration and evaluation

Developing written response skills

When you answer a question on short stories, you need to show that your response is dealing with essential GCSE skills and linked to details of the text.

You will need to do this in a focused way when writing in the exam, making your points about two stories quickly and linking your chosen textual detail to a clear purpose.

The following examples can be used and adapted to help you develop these writing skills. Every sentence has to count!

Writer's purpose

I think he/she wants the reader to feel / to make the reader think / to show that …
The writer was writing to explore a familiar relationship in an unusual way by …
The end of the story lets the reader understand / leaves the reader wondering …

Ideas and perspectives

This creates the idea that she/he may have …
This is a gloomy/optimistic/sympathetic way of looking at life because …
She writes this because she thinks that …

Interpretation and relevance to me or others

I think the writer wrote this story because she wanted to …
I think this is a good way of showing how …
There are two ways of looking at this, such as …

Language

The words that create this mood are …
The writer uses dialogue to show feelings and attitudes, such as …
The writer uses language that is realistic but also symbolic, as in …

Structure and form

The story starts with a description of a normal, comfortable setting/relationship but there are hints that there is something else beneath the surface, such as …
The story is structured as a slow revealing of a truth, with hints along the way …
The narrator is a character in the story, which makes the reader feel that …

Contexts

I wouldn't do that, but if I was in that situation, maybe I would because…
The writer makes you realise how much a culture influences what a person thinks and does …
The story reflects some of the social conditions and ideas about society that …

MODERN SHORT STORIES IN THE EXAM

Your GCSE English Literature course has been designed so that you read a range of literature including Shakespeare, a 19th-century novel, poetry from 1789 to the present day and modern texts.

At the end of your GCSE course in English Literature you will sit an exam. The Literature exam has two papers:

- **Paper 1: Shakespeare and the 19th-century novel**, which is worth 40% of your GCSE.
- **Paper 2: Modern texts and poetry**, which is worth 60% of your GCSE.

Paper 2: Modern texts and poetry has three sections:

- **Section A: Modern texts**, where you answer **one** essay question from a choice of two on your studied modern prose or drama text – in this case, the Short Story Anthology, *Telling Tales*. You will need to write about **two** short stories.

- **Section B: Poetry**, where you answer one question on comparing poems from your chosen cluster of the anthology, 'Love and relationships' **or** 'Power and conflict'.
- **Section C: Unseen poetry**, where you write about a poem that you have not seen before and then compare this poem with a second unseen poem.

GCSE English Literature assessment objectives

The assessment objectives (AOs) form the basis for the GCSE mark scheme. For Paper 2, Section A, the assessment of your response to two short stories is against four assessment objectives:

AO1: Read, understand and respond to texts. Students should be able to:

- maintain a critical style and develop an informed personal response
- use textual references, including quotations, to support and illustrate interpretations.

AO2: Analyse the language, form and structure used by a writer to create meanings and effects, using relevant subject terminology where appropriate.

AO3: Show understanding of the relationships between texts and the contexts in which they were written.

AO4: Use a range of vocabulary and sentence structures for clarity, purpose and effect, with accurate spelling and punctuation.

The AO3 'contexts' may include also the context in which a story is set, literary contexts such as genres, and the context of different audiences, including you in the 21st century.

Organising your response to exam questions

In your examination you have to write about two stories. Your exam question will give you a focus for writing about one named story. The focus may be discovery, change, feelings, relationships (the

'What'), but it will also be on the way the stories are written (the 'How'). You have to write about that story and that focus; then choose another story to write about with a linked focus.

You can organise your response in many ways. Some examples are given below.

a   The simplest way could be to write a response in two halves. In this case you would:

- first, write about the named story
- then write about the chosen story
- link each part of the response to the question focus.

b   You could adapt the above simple model in the following way:

- introduce both stories , with a focus on the link
- develop your response by writing about themes, ideas and the writer's craft in the named story, then in your chosen story
- include your personal response at the end, based on your own interest, preference or thoughts arising from your study.

c   You could adapt the above model further in the following way:

- introduce both stories, with a focus on the link
- develop your response by writing about both stories together, first the themes and ideas in both stories, then the writers' craft in both stories
- include your personal response at the end, based on your own interest, preference or thoughts arising from your study.

When writing about both stories, you might choose to compare them. If so, you will be assessed on your response to the question and the themes, ideas and writer's craft for each story, not on your comparison. Comparing is, however, an effective way of organising your writing to show your insight and response – which are rewarded.

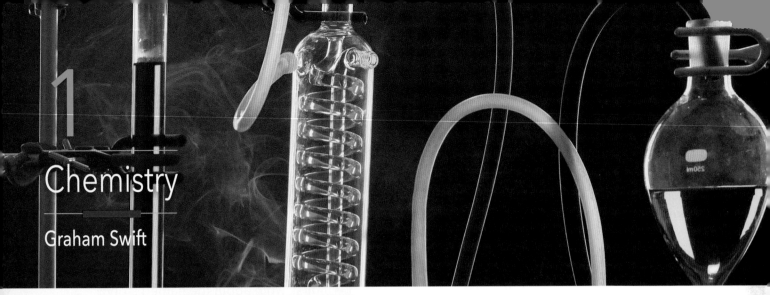

1 Chemistry

Graham Swift

Your progress in this unit:

- explore how Graham Swift presents the thoughts and feelings of the characters
- develop your own interpretation of characters, relationships and events
- understand how Swift presents themes and ideas
- explore and analyse how Swift's use of language and structure affects the reader
- practise and develop your written response skills.

GETTING STARTED – THE STORY AND YOU

1 How many meanings of the word 'chemistry' can you think of? Work with a partner to jot down ideas.

2 Match these three quotations to the people who you think said them.

Jim-al-Khalili

Stephen Hawking

I wanted to do math and physics, but my father made me do chemistry because he thought there would be no jobs for mathematicians.

We've all seen great actors and actresses who are missing a certain chemistry. And it's not about getting along or not getting along.

Johnny Galecki

The explosive story of chemistry is the story of the building blocks that make up our entire world – the elements. From fiery phosphorous to the pure untarnished lustre of gold and the dazzle of violent, violet potassium, everything is made of elements.

STORY ESSENTIALS

Who

Major characters
The boy
His mother
His grandfather
Ralph, the new man in the mother's life

Minor characters
Alec, the boy's father, now dead
Vera, the boy's grandmother, now dead

When and where

The events take place in the late 20th century. The story is set at a pond in a park, in the boy's home and in Grandfather's shed.

Sequence of events

- The young boy, his mother and his grandfather live together after the deaths of the boy's father and his grandmother. The three of them are united in grief but have a reasonably contented life.
- This is disrupted by the arrival of Ralph, a physically big man who is clearly determined to get his way.
- Grandfather spends more and more time in his shed, engaged in his hobby – experimenting with chemicals.
- The boy hates Ralph so much that he takes some acid from the shed and means to throw it in Ralph's face the next morning. This is prevented by Grandfather's suicide.
- The story ends with the family preparing to move house. There is nowhere else for the boy to go.

Themes and ideas

- grief
- guilt
- loneliness

- narrative voice
- relationships
- hatred

- ageing
- power
- how some things do not end

Contexts

Graham Swift was born in London in 1949. He wrote 'Chemistry' in 1982. As well as short stories, he has written a number of novels, including *Last Orders*, which won the Booker Prize in 1996 and was made into a film in 2001.

I often write about the moments of crisis in people's lives where a space opens up and it's strange because I think I identify with that quite strongly. But I am a very fortunate individual, I'm lucky I discovered what I wanted to do with my life and I am doing it, so I'm fulfilled and there aren't many people who can say that.

GETTING CLOSER – FOCUS ON DETAILS

The following activities will help you develop your skills from understanding to interpreting. As you work through this unit, you will also progress from exploring to analysing the story. Keep your own notes as you work through the activities. You will use them to bring together your written response to the story at the end of the unit.

What happens in the story?

We understand what happens in the story from the point of view of the boy, who is writing when he has grown up.

1 Choose four points in the story and write diary entries from the mother's point of view. Include:

a   what has happened
b   what she feels about this.

2 Working in a small group, hot-seat the characters of Mother and Ralph and explore what happens in the story from their point of view. For example you might want to know what Ralph thinks about Grandfather's protective attitude to the boy's mother or what the mother thinks about her son's behaviour.

Understanding the characters

Chemistry is the science of change.

🔊 **Listen to an extract from the story on Cambridge Elevate.**

The writer's use of detail helps you to feel familiar with aspects of a character. This is something that you will need to learn to identify and comment on. Start with the facts in the story.

1 Read the first paragraph of the story. Then answer these questions.

a   What impression do you have of the relationships between Grandfather, Mother and the boy? What evidence can you find in the text to suggest this? Create a table to help organise your ideas. For example:

Statement	Evidence
They relied on each other.	
Grandfather dominated them.	'As if Grandfather were pulling us towards him on some invisible cord'
They enjoyed each other's company.	
They did not want other people to disturb them.	
They had become a self-contained unit.	

b   The motor-launch is important in the first section. What do you think it might suggest about their relationships?

2 The character of Ralph is introduced soon after this point in the story.

   a Read the paragraph that begins 'It was some months …'. What impression of Ralph do you have from this paragraph?

   b What do you learn about his relationships with the other characters?

3 Complete a table to show what evidence you can find in the story to support these statements about Ralph. For example:

Ralph	
Statement	**Evidence**
He wants the boy to like him.	*His offer to get the boy a new boat is described 'as if pouncing on something', which shows his eagerness.*
He is short-tempered.	
He is used to getting his own way.	
He is greedy.	
He is determined to be the alpha male in the house.	

 4 Now create a similar table for the character of the mother. Think of five statements about her, and find evidence to support each one.

Where does the story happen?

The writer's choice of a **setting** is important in any story. In this section you will consider how the writer makes the setting believable.

 1 Read this extract from the last paragraph in the story. What impression do you get of the pond in the park?

> I had nowhere to go. I went down to the park and stood by the pond. Dead willow leaves floated on it. Beneath its surface was a bottle of acid and the wreck of my launch.

2 Now look at the description of the pond at the start of the story. Write notes about:

   a the layout
   b the season
   c the effect of the wind
   d the privacy it allows.

3 Do you think it is a pleasant place? Give reasons for your answer.

> **🔑 Key terms**
>
> **setting:** the description of the place in which a story is set.

13

> We would go even in the winter ... when the leaves on the two willows turned yellow and dropped and the water froze your hands.

Themes and ideas

The early part of the story brings out the ideas of loss, grief and being mutually supportive. The self-reliance of the small family is disrupted by the arrival of a fourth character, Ralph, who quickly becomes dominant.

The boy feels that his way of life is now being threatened and that the quiet contentment of his family will be destroyed.

Working with a partner, discuss the following questions.

1 When the boat sinks, Grandfather says:

'You must accept it – you can't get it back – it's the only way'

a What do you think he is really talking about?
b When she hears this, the mother's face is described as '**very still and very white, as if she had seen something appalling**'. Why do you think she reacts like this?
c The narrator describes the family as living '**within the scope of this sad symmetry**'. What do you think he means by this?

2 In the paragraph beginning 'My father's death was a far less remote event than my grandmother's …', the narrator makes a distinction between adult and childish grief. What do you think are the distinctions?

PUTTING DETAILS TO USE

Now that you have looked at the story more closely, you can use the details you have discovered to build the important skills you will need to explore the key areas of character, setting and ideas.

Exploring the characters, setting, ideas and feelings

1 What evidence can you find to support the following interpretations of the boy's personality?

a He is lonely.
b He is imaginative.
c He feels his world is threatened.
d He loves his mother and wishes to protect her.
e He loves his grandfather and feels sorry for him.
f He is ruthless.
g He feels he can explain his grandfather's suicide.

2 A student was asked to write about the character of Ralph. This is what they wrote:

> *Ralph is a natural destroyer: he successfully destroys the fragile family unit. His size alone makes him seem threatening. The narrator notes that 'he liked his food' and later that he was eating 'bigger and bigger meals'. He is also shown as something of a sexual predator, 'his big lurching frame almost enveloping' the mother. By the end of the story he has completely replaced the father, even wearing one of his old sweaters. He has managed to 'penetrate' what the boy describes as 'that old impregnable domain' of his family. It is no surprise that the mother and Ralph are planning to move to a new house and, presumably, to marry.*

Using this interpretation of Ralph as an example, write three sentences in response to each of the following tasks:

a   Describe, with supporting details, what the character of the mother is like.
b   Describe, with supporting details, the grandfather's shed.
c   Describe some of the strong feelings and attitudes shown by the boy, for example his hatred of Ralph and his failure to understand death.

The narrator's standpoint

As you read the stories in *Telling Tales*, you will find that some are **third-person narratives** (see for example 'Odour of Chrysanthemums' in Unit 2). Usually, the person telling the story knows everything about every character, and can move from one setting to another whenever they wish to.

'Chemistry' is a **first-person narrative**. The narrator is an adult, possibly even an old man, looking back on the events of his childhood and giving a frank and honest insight into what he thought and felt when he was a young boy. The reader sees the events through the narrator's eyes. The other characters might have a different **viewpoint** and a completely different way of thinking about what happened.

Watch an expert discuss key themes and ideas in the story on Cambridge Elevate.

Learning checkpoint

Select three quotations from the text that helped you to form an opinion of one of the following:

- a character
- the setting for the story
- a feeling or attitude.

Write a sentence to explain how each of the quotations supports your interpretation.

Key terms

third-person narrative: an account of events using 'he', 'she' or 'they', rather than 'I' or 'we'.
first-person narrative: an account of events written from a personal point of view (so using 'I' or 'we' rather than 'he', 'she' or 'they').
viewpoint: the position from which a character sees things.

What the characters say and do

In order to make a character believable for the reader, the writer has to give enough information about what the character says and does.

Look at this extract from the opening paragraph of the story:

For some reason it was always Grandfather, never I, who went to the far side. When he reached his station I would hear his 'Ready!' across the water. A puff of vapour would rise from his lips like the smoke from a muffled pistol. And I would release the launch … As it moved it seemed that it followed an actual existing line between Grandfather, myself and Mother, as if Grandfather were pulling us towards him on some invisible cord, and that he had to do this to prove we were not beyond his reach. When the boat drew near him he would crouch on his haunches. His hands – which I knew were knotted, veiny and mottled from an accident in one of his chemical experiments – would reach out, grasp it and set it on its return.

In this paragraph, Swift creates an impression of the characters of both the boy and his grandfather, and of the relationship between the three characters.

1 Working in a pair, **annotate** a copy of these lines to show how Swift has used language to suggest the passage is written by an individual. Think about:

a   how the family is presented as a self-contained unit
b   the physical description of Grandfather's hands (what effect does this have on the reader?)
c   words or phrases that suggest Grandfather wants to be the most important person in the family.

🔑 Key terms

annotate: to write notes on a text to highlight details.
dialogue: where two or more characters are speaking to each other.

A puff of vapour would rise from his lips like the smoke from a muffled pistol.

2 Make a copy of the following table. How does what Grandfather says reveal aspects of his feelings and attitudes? The first point has been completed for you as an example.

Quotation	Grandfather's feelings and attitudes
'You must accept it – you can't get it back – it's the only way'	*Grandfather is still feeling the loss of his wife and is trying to accept it. He understands that death must be accepted as being a part of life.*
'Leave her alone? What do you know about being left alone?'	
'You don't make curry any more, the way you did for Alec, the way Vera taught you.'	
'I thought you would come.'	
'Anything can change. Even gold can change.'	
'They change. But the elements don't change.'	
'Laurel water. Prussic acid. Not for drinking.'	

How the characters relate to each other

Writers may also use **dialogue** to give readers an understanding of characters and relationships. The way people speak to each other can reveal a lot about themselves and the way they see others.

Swift puts some ideas and attitudes into his characters' mouths that indicate their own attitudes and feelings, for example their attitudes to Grandfather. He does this by allowing the boy to witness these incidents.

1 With a partner, explain what you think each of the following quotations reveals about the other characters' attitudes towards Grandfather. One quotation has already been completed as an example.

Quotation about Grandfather	What this reveals about the speaker's feelings and attitudes towards him
Ralph: 'Why don't you leave her alone?!'	
Ralph: 'For Christ's sake we're not waiting all night for him to finish! Get the pudding!'	
Mother: 'You're ruining our meal – do you want to take yours out to your shed?!'	
Mother: 'Grandpa was old and ill, he wouldn't have lived much longer anyway.'	*She is showing that she is glad, or at least relieved, that he is dead and treats his death as being of little consequence.*
Mother: 'There – isn't that lovely?'	

Exploring themes and ideas

There are many references to loss, grief and change in the story. The narrator makes a distinction between the grief experienced by a child and that experienced by an adult, and tries to understand how people can change.

 1 Explore ideas about how important the loss of Vera is to Grandfather by answering the following questions.

    a   What does he do and what does he refuse to do?

    b   In what ways does Grandfather choose to remember her?

    c   Why do you think these are significant?

2 What impression do you get of the way the boy's mother reacts to the loss of her husband, Alec? Think about:

    a   what she says and does

    b   what she does **not** do

    c   why these things have a significance in the story (for example the food and the sweater).

3 Swift uses ghosts as a part of the story. The ghosts of the boy's father and grandfather both appear to him.

    a   What do you think is important about what his father tells the boy?

    b   What does this suggest to the reader about how the boy now views his mother?

    c   Why do you think Swift repeats the image of the pools of water?

    d   Why does what happens when the boy wakes up make the placing of this ghostly visitation important at this point in the story?

4 The following examples of students' work show how you can develop your **understanding** into **interpretation** to **explore** other possible meanings. What differences do you notice in the three answers, in response to the following question?

What is the significance of the father's ghost?

He appears to the boy dripping wet and with seaweed on his shoulders because the boy thinks he has stayed on the bottom of the Irish Sea.

> Shows understanding

The boy sees his father's ghost because he is so upset with his mother and Ralph. He does not usually go to sleep before he sees Grandfather's light is off because he feels that he is watching over him. The ghost then appears and accuses his mother of causing the boat to sink and his plane to crash. It is all the mother's fault.

> Shows interpretation

The appearance of the father's ghost shows the boy's innocence and lack of understanding of death: the salt and seaweed indicate that the boy believed his father, like his grandmother, was 'at the bottom of the Irish Sea' and wanted to know 'when he would return'. That he then suggests that perhaps he knows his father would not return shows he is gradually beginning to understand death. His father's ghost clearly shows that on some level the boy has understood that the boat's sinking is linked to the breakdown of the family. The ghost links the boat and the plane crash and the repeated 'Don't you believe me?' may be read as being a plea for revenge. The reader is left wondering what the 'something' is that was pulling him towards the door: does he have only a brief time or is he now moving from the Irish Sea to somewhere else or nowhere?

> Shows exploration

Analysing language

When you analyse a story, you should look closely at different parts of the story to see how they are connected. These may form a pattern. Often, close study of the language may reveal details of the author's meanings and purposes that on a first reading you may not have noticed. These details are usually called **implications**.

What someone says can be taken as a fact or as a sign of something more – a feeling, an attitude or a personality trait. **Implied meaning** can be different from what is apparently being said.

Writers choose their words to convey a range of things – usually ideas, feelings and attitudes. Sometimes even a short and simple sentence can show how a writer has chosen words carefully.

1 Mother says to Grandfather: **'You're ruining our meal – do you want to take yours out to your shed?!'** Rank the following statements according to how close you think they are to what the mother means in this sentence, giving reasons for your decisions:

a She does not want to wait for her pudding.
b She wants to get rid of Grandfather so she can enjoy the meal with Ralph.
c She does not want the crumble to go cold.
d She wants to tell Grandfather that she now values Ralph more than him.
e She thinks she should do what Ralph wants her to do.

Sometimes language is used to give us **facts** and an accurate description of something. At other times it is used just to create an **impression**.

2 Writers can sometimes pack a lot of meaning into a very short phrase, for example when Swift writes about Ralph:

You see, he liked his food.

This might appear a strange excuse for his ordering of the pudding but Swift highlights the point by giving the sentence a paragraph to itself.

a Why do you think Swift uses the phrase **'You see'**?
b What else might Ralph's liking of food imply?
c What other moments in the story associate Ralph with food?
d Why do you think Swift includes them?

It is important that you develop your skills in analysing the language used by the writer. The purpose of this is to gather together details to see if you can identify patterns in them, or understand how they may relate to each other. For example a physical detail may represent something more than what it literally is.

3 Discuss the following quotations from the story about the weather and the natural world. Make notes to help you answer the following question: **How might the weather and the natural world be related to what different characters are feeling?**

When the wind blew, little waves travelled across it and slapped the paved edges.

The leaves on the two willows turned yellow and dropped.

the evergreen shrubs which filled our garden were defying the onset of autumn. Only the cherry-laurel bushes were partly denuded

All that autumn was exceptionally cold.

rain was dashing against the window as if the house were plunging under water.

The heavy rain and the tossing branches of a rowan tree obscured my view.

It was a brilliant, crisp late November day and the leaves on the rowan tree were all gold.

They tidied the overgrown parts of the garden and clipped back the trees.

The air was very cold.

Symbolism

Sometimes a writer uses words or actions in a way that gives them a wider meaning. In this story, we can find **symbolism** in the study and practice of chemistry. For example the following extract by a student describes how the apple crumble is used as a symbol:

The apple crumble is 'seething', which is exactly what the relationships in the house are like at that moment. Not only is everyone angry or upset or both, but their emotions are about to overflow, just like the 'burnt sugar and apple juice'.

1 Discuss and make notes about the following questions.

a Grandfather says: '**You don't make things in chemistry – you change them. Anything can change.**' Do you think he is speaking about chemistry or relationships?

b Why does Grandfather say, '**Then we'd take something that wasn't gold at all and cover it with this changed gold so it looked as if it was all gold – but it wasn't.**'?

c Why does Grandfather not put the watch chain into the beaker?

d What does the boy mean when he thinks '**how suicide can be murder and how things don't end**'?

e In the final paragraph, the boy thinks '**But though things change they aren't destroyed**'. What do you think is the signifcance of this?

But though things change
they aren't destroyed.

Exploring a key moment in the story

The moment when the ambulance arrives to take away the dead grandfather is an important point in the story. The boy watches from a bedroom window as Ralph appears outside the house and seems to be supervising the paramedics.

 1 Re-read the paragraph beginning 'And then it was almost light …' and then make notes on:

a how the weather contributes to the drama of what is happening
b how the boy's view is obscured so he does not understand what is happening
c how Ralph appears to be an almost comic figure
d how Ralph also appears to have some authority
e the boy's reaction when he realises what is happening
f the importance of the smell of whisky
g the mother's promise of an explanation.

Analysing structure

1 The story begins and ends at the pond. Why do you think Swift does this?

Working in a small group, rank the following statements according to how well you think they answer this question. Explain your decisions.

The story begins and ends at the pond to:

a suggest that the boy is lonely
b remind the reader of the bottle of acid and the boy's dislike of Ralph
c show that Graham Swift likes to include water in his stories
d remind the reader of the lost boat and the changes that have happened in the family
e show that the boy wishes to return to somewhere where he felt loved
f show that things don't change, even after death.

 2 Re-read the last paragraph of the story. Then answer these questions.

a What details can you find that create a sad **atmosphere**?
b In what ways does the description of the grandfather link to the opening of the story?

🔑 **Key terms**

symbolism: the use of one thing to represent another.
atmosphere: the feeling created by a writer's description of a setting.

✔ **Learning checkpoint**

Use what you have learnt so far in this unit to answer the following questions.

1 Annotate the last two sentences to explore their meaning. What do you think Swift wants the reader to learn from these sentences?

He was smiling and I knew: the launch was still travelling over to him, unstoppable, unsinkable, along that invisible line. And his hands, his acid-marked hands, would reach out to receive it.

2 Which of the following best describes how you feel about the ending of the story?

sad	hopeful	celebratory
uplifting	curious	sentimental

3 Why do you think the story is called 'Chemistry'?

GETTING IT INTO WRITING

As you have worked through this unit, you have built on your understanding by analysing and interpreting the text. You will now have the opportunity to develop your ideas into a written response. Remember: in your examination, you will be asked to write about **two** stories, but here you will focus on just one.

 Use your exploration of the story, and the notes you have taken, to write a response of no more than 300 words to the following question:

> How does Swift present the relationships between characters in 'Chemistry'?
>
> Write about:
>
> - how Swift presents the relationship between two characters in the story
> - how Swift uses the characters to explore the themes of grief and change.

When writing your response to this question, remember to:

- include details of how the story develops
- use short quotations to support your ideas
- explore implied meanings (the ideas behind the words)
- identify different viewpoints
- give your own personal response.

Complete this assignment on Cambridge Elevate.

Structuring your response

Using the work you have already done in this unit as a starting point, write about **four** relationships in the story. You should aim to write at least one paragraph about each of these relationships.

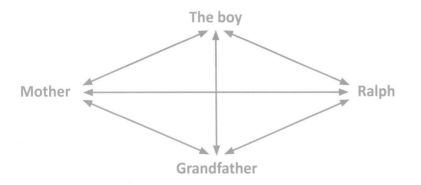

It may help if you think of the question as a 'What' and a 'How' – **What** is the story about? **How** is it written?

The 'What' is the feelings and attitudes in the story, for example grief and change.

The 'How' is the writer's way of conveying those things through language and use of language devices.

> Often I could not sleep until … I knew that Grandfather had shuffled back to the house and slipped in, like a stray cat

For the **first** part, you will need to:

- bring together the notes you made earlier in this unit to illustrate the feelings of the boy, his mother and his grandfather towards their losses
- illustrate how these feelings change over the course of the story
- examine their relationships in detail – for example how things in the family change or stay the same and how the characters feel at the end of the story.

For the **second** part, you will need to show how Swift uses his craft as a writer through language and symbolism to:

- show the characters' feelings and attitudes
- represent ideas about how people respond to, and try to cope with, grief.

Improving your response

1 Here are some extracts from students' responses to the question about the relationships in the story. Work with a partner to decide which extracts have gone beyond simple comments about the story to a convincing exploration of language or ideas.

Student A

The boy clearly does not like Ralph as he is taking his father's place. He does not want Ralph to buy him a new boat and says no several times to try to show

Ralph that he will never accept him. Later in the story he wants to 'spoil his face' so that his mother 'would no longer want him'.

Student B

Swift shows that the boy feels great sympathy for his grandfather's situation. The boy is aware that the shed provides the grandfather with 'a sealed-off world', which shows that the grandfather is in need of a place where he can feel some security and 'solace', not just from the loss of his wife but also from the potential loss of his daughter and the quiet happiness they had shared when he provided for her. Now the boy is sorry that his grandfather looks like 'some torpid captive animal' and slips into the house 'like a stray cat'. In the boy's eyes, Grandfather is becoming a poor, hunted animal.

Student C

The relationship between the mother and Ralph develops throughout the story. The first important moment is when she gives Ralph the apple-crumble and says to Grandfather, 'You're ruining our meal'. She has sided with Ralph because she is making Grandfather leave the house to eat on his own. She is making stews for Ralph and not curries for the grandfather, so she is obviously showing that she now feels more for Ralph than for Grandfather.

Student D

The boy in the story does not like his mother's new boyfriend, Ralph, and plans to throw acid in his face so his mother will not want him anymore. His plan is stopped when his grandfather commits suicide by drinking a poison that he has made in his shed.

Student E

Swift implies that the narrator seemed to have been satisfied with the 'sad symmetry' of grief in which he, his mother and his grandfather had found themselves. The narrator writes that they lived 'quietly, calmly, even contentedly'. Here the word 'even' appears to suggest that this was something of a surprise. The same is true of his judgement that for a year 'we were really quite happy'. Again the word 'quite' indicates that whatever happiness was to be had in their mutual relationships was something of a small triumph.

Student F

Perhaps the most intriguing relationship in the story is that of the narrator and his younger self. Swift emphasises that the narrator was only ten years old at the time, but some of the boy's thoughts and feelings seem to be too mature for one so young. For example the narrator reveals that he wanted to tell the policemen and officials from the coroner's court 'a thousand things' – clearly this is a hyperbolic response. He continues that he wanted to explain 'how suicide can be murder and how things don't end'. This level of subtlety is unlikely in one so young, however sensitive and intelligent, and seems to be the narrator projecting his later feelings on his ten-year-old self. The clue may be in the statement that his mother, alive at the time of writing, 'has been trying to explain, or to avoid explaining' since the suicide.

2 Having thought about these extracts, go back to your own response. What could you do to improve it?

GETTING FURTHER

1 Imagine you are going to adapt the story into a comic-strip format. Think about the following questions.

   a   If you were only allowed ten images, which would you choose?

   b   What captions or speech would you include?

   c   Now take this a stage further and **storyboard** a trailer for a television drama adaptation of the story.

2 Script or improvise a role-playing scene in which the boy, now an old man, is questioned about his childhood by a psychiatrist.

> **Key terms**
>
> **storyboard:** to make a sequence of drawings that show the different scenes in a story.

And his hands, his acid-marked hands, would reach out to receive it.

2

Odour of Chrysanthemums

D.H. Lawrence

Your progress in this unit:

- explore how D.H. Lawrence presents the thoughts and feelings of the characters
- develop your own interpretation of details about characters, relationships and events
- understand how Lawrence presents themes and ideas
- explore and analyse how Lawrence's use of language and structure affects the reader
- develop your written response skills.

GETTING STARTED – THE STORY AND YOU

These photographs of coal miners were taken in the same area in which the story is set and around the same time. What do they tell you? What do you think life would have been like for these miners?

These miners worked at Brinsley Colliery, the **setting** for 'Odour of Chrysanthemums'. The picture was taken in 1913 – just two years after Lawrence wrote the story.

This image from a Nottinghamshire colliery shows miners in a pit cage. This was pulled up and down by a winding-engine like the one mentioned in the story.

This picture of a pit pony pulling a cart full of coal was also taken at Brinsley Colliery. How old do you think the miner leading the pony might be?

STORY ESSENTIALS

Who

Major characters
Elizabeth Bates
Walter Bates, her husband
Annie and John, her children
Her mother-in-law

Minor characters
Elizabeth's father, an engine driver
Mr and Mrs Rigley, neighbours
Mr Matthews, the manager of the pit
A collier and a doctor

When and where

The setting is a small cottage near Brinsley Colliery, Nottinghamshire, in the early 1900s.

Sequence of events

- A train stops by a cottage near a mine. The driver and his daughter, Elizabeth, discuss his forthcoming marriage and her husband Walter, who is a heavy drinker.
- Elizabeth prepares the family tea and she and her two children wait for Walter's return but he does not come.
- Elizabeth goes to look for her husband and asks the Rigleys for help. She returns home.
- Walter's mother arrives with the news that Walter has been killed in a terrible mining accident.
- The pit manager and some helpers bring Walter's body and lay it in the parlour.
- Elizabeth and Walter's mother wash and clothe the body.
- Elizabeth thinks about her marriage, life and death, and the ways in which people never really know each other.

Themes and ideas

- death
- grief
- lack of love
- loneliness
- marriage
- narrative voice
- change
- disillusion
- how the present affects the future

ⓘ Contexts

D.H. Lawrence (1885–1930) was the son of a coal miner and grew up in Nottinghamshire, the setting for this short story, which he wrote in 1911. He is best known for his novels, such as *Sons and Lovers*, *Women in Love* and the controversial *Lady Chatterley's Lover*, which was banned in Britain until 1960, but he also wrote short stories, poems, essays and plays.

The real joy of a book lies in reading it over and over again, and always finding something different, coming upon another meaning, another level of meaning. It is, as usual, a question of values: we are so overwhelmed with quantities of books, that we hardly realise any more that a book can be valuable, valuable like a jewel, or a lovely picture, into which you can look deeper and deeper and get a more profound experience every time. It is far, far better to read one book six times, at intervals, than to read six several books.

GETTING CLOSER – FOCUS ON DETAILS

The following activities will help you develop your skills from understanding to interpreting. As you work through this unit, you will also progress from exploring to analysing the story. Keep your own notes as you work through the activities. You will use them to bring together your written response to the story at the end of the unit.

What happens in the story?

1 Imagine that you are a film director and wish to turn the story into a film. You only have the budget to shoot six scenes.

    a Which six scenes would you choose?

    b How will you justify your decisions?

2 Working in a small group, hot-seat the characters of Mr and Mrs Rigley and Mr Matthews and explore what happens in the story from their point of view. Ask them about:

    a their meeting with Elizabeth and what they did to try to help her

    b their opinions about the Bates family

    c their reactions on hearing the news of Walter's death.

Work in a group of three. Two of you are going to act and one will be the director. (Remember: the role of the director is to help the actors think about what they might say, and then advise them so that their performance is as realistic and truthful as possible.)

3 Imagine that Annie and John meet many years later at their mother's funeral.

    a Act out their meeting.

    b Discuss what led up to their father's death and how it affected their family.

    c Suggest what might have happened to them subsequently.

Understanding the characters

Lawrence's use of detail helps the reader to get to know the characters in the story.

1 Read from the end of the third paragraph ('She closed and padlocked the door …') down to the point when Elizabeth's father leaves and she goes back indoors ('Her husband did not come.')

🔊 **Listen to an extract from the story on Cambridge Elevate.**

Just beyond rose the tapering chimneys and the clumsy black headstocks of Brinsley Colliery.

a   What impression do you have of the relationship between Elizabeth Bates and her son John? What evidence can you find in the text to suggest this? Complete a table like the following one:

Statement	Evidence
She worries about his safety.	
She often tells John off.	'I thought you were down at that wet brook – and you remember what I told you'
She tries to be kind to him.	
He does not enjoy his mother's company.	
He rarely speaks to his mother.	

b   What impression do you have of the relationship between Elizabeth Bates and her father? What evidence can you find in the text to suggest this? Complete a table like the following one:

Statement	Evidence
She is kind to him.	
She is not pleased he is going to be married.	
He wants her to approve of his marriage.	'It's no sort of life for a man of my years, to sit at my own hearth like a stranger.'
He enjoys her company.	
He does not like it when she contradicts him.	

2   Copy and complete the following table to show what evidence you can find in the story to support these statements about Walter.

Walter	
Statement	Evidence
He hates the cold.	
He was charming and handsome when he was young.	
He drinks too much.	
He does not seem to care about his family.	He spends half a sovereign (ten shillings) on drink and only gives his wife twenty-three shillings for the housekeeping.
He hates his way of life.	

3   Now complete a similar table for Annie Bates. Think of five statements about her and find a piece of evidence to support each one.

Where does the story happen?

The writer's choice of a setting is important in any story. In this section you will consider how Lawrence makes the setting of this story realistic and believable.

1 Make a copy of this mind map of the Bates's cottage and then add your own notes around the four headings.

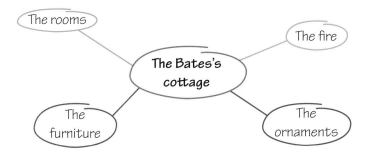

How homely a place is it? Give reasons for your answer.

2 Read the description of the area around the cottage at the start of the story. Write notes about:

a   the spinney
b   the weather
c   the fields
d   the railway lines
e   the view in the distance.

3 To what extent is it a pleasant place? Give reasons for your answer.

Themes and ideas

In the last seven paragraphs of the story, Elizabeth tries to come to terms with the sudden death of her husband. She is now a widow with two children and a third on the way. She no longer has any form of income and her future, and that of her children, is uncertain.

She feels sorrow that he died a dreadful death and has a horror of his dead body. She also feels something else – a sense that she never really knew the man she had married and who was the father of her children.

1 Find three sentences from different paragraphs that show Elizabeth realises she never really knew her husband.

2 Look at the following list of themes. With a partner, discuss what you think is the main theme of the story. Give reasons for your choice. You can adapt a theme or write your own if none of these seem to fit.

a   Accidents can happen when you least expect them.
b   A sudden death can destroy a family.
c   Marriage can sometimes bring happiness (for example for Elizabeth's father) and sometimes unhappiness (for example for Elizabeth).
d   You can never fully know another person – ultimately we are all alone in the world.
e   Alcohol can have tragic effects.

PUTTING DETAILS TO USE

Now that you have looked at the story more closely, you can use the details you have discovered to build the important skills you will need to explore the key areas of character, setting and ideas.

Exploring the characters, setting, ideas and feelings

1 What evidence can you find to support the following interpretations of the character of Walter's mother?

a   She thinks her son was a good lad when he was young.
b   She realises that he behaved badly towards his wife and children.
c   She tries to excuse his behaviour and make allowances for him.
d   She is deeply pessimistic by nature.
e   She mourns her dead son in a highly dramatic way.
f   She retreats into her own world when her son's corpse is brought in.
g   She finds a kind of beauty in her son's corpse.

2 A student was asked to write about the character of Walter's mother. This is what they wrote:

Walter's mother mourns his death in a melodramatic way, which provides a very sharp contrast to the stoical and practical attitude shown, at any rate on the surface, by Elizabeth who is the one who organises the laying out and washing of the body and ensures that the parlour door is locked so that her children cannot see their father. The mother, who is variously described as the 'old woman', 'elder woman' and 'old mother' seems to be mourning her son as she remembers him when he was a lad with 'a hearty laugh'. She seems to have little connection with the man he has become.

Using this interpretation of Walter's mother as an example, write three sentences in response to each of the following tasks:

a   Describe, with supporting details, the character of Elizabeth Bates.
b   Describe, with supporting details, the setting of the Bates's cottage and its surroundings.
c   Describe some of the strong feelings and attitudes shown by Elizabeth, for example her feelings towards her husband both before and after she knows of his death.

✔ Learning checkpoint

Select three quotations from the text that helped you to form an opinion of one of the following:

- a character
- the setting for the story
- a feeling or attitude.

Write a sentence to explain how each of the quotations supports your interpretation.

 Watch an expert discuss key themes and ideas from the story on Cambridge Elevate.

they curved away towards the coppice where the withered oak leaves dropped noiselessly

The narrator's standpoint

In 'Chemistry', Graham Swift wrote from the perspective of the boy, now an adult, remembering what happened and how he felt about his situation. This was an example of a **first-person narrative**.

This story is a **third-person narrative**. Lawrence describes what happens as if he is outside the story. What we know about the characters comes from how he describes them and the ways in which they behave and interact. The narrator does not appear as a character in the story and knows everything about what happens: he is an **omniscient** narrator.

However, there is one exception to this rule. Lawrence does tell us what Elizabeth Bates is thinking and feeling, for example her thoughts on her husband's drinking and her devastation when his body is brought back to their house.

What the characters say and do

Lawrence describes Elizabeth as a striking woman:

> She was a tall woman of imperious mien, handsome, with definite black eyebrows. Her smooth black hair was parted exactly.

The '**imperious mien**' (her commanding expression) and the fact that her parting is exact show that she is a woman who is proud of herself and careful in what she does. The reader's first impression of her is that she is a strong woman.

1 What evidence you can find that Elizabeth:

   a   talks in a different way to the other people in the story

   b   looks down on Mrs Rigley's house

   c   tries to make her own house comfortable

   d   looks after her husband

   e   disapproves of her father

   f   dislikes her mother-in-law

   g   is a good mother

   h   considers herself to be superior to the others in the story?

2 If you were asked to describe Elizabeth to someone who had not read the story, how would you sum her up in one minute?

Exploring themes and ideas

1 Four students were asked what they thought was the most important theme of 'Odour of Chrysanthemums'. They replied:

> It's about the ways marriage can be destructive: the women have to rely on their husbands for money and stability and so become trapped in a loveless relationship.

> It's about how a sudden and completely unexpected event can shake your life, and things can never be the same again.

> It's about how fear can affect a whole family: all the characters are prevented from changing their relationships because they are afraid of each other.

> It's about how people sometimes never understand each other: at the end of the story Elizabeth realises that she has been married to a man she has never really known.

Work with a partner. What evidence from the story do you think these four students could give to support their ideas?

Key terms

omniscient: all-seeing and all-knowing. The omniscient narrator of a story knows more than the reader about the situation and how it will develop.

2 What do you think the main theme(s) of the story are? You can choose more than one from the students' suggestions in Question 1, or suggest your own, but ensure you can back up your choices with evidence from the story.

3 The following examples of students' work show how you can develop your **understanding** into **interpretation** to **explore** other possible meanings. What differences do you notice in the three answers, in response to the following question:

What realisation does Elizabeth have at the end of the story?

She realises that she and Walter were strangers in their own home. Even though she was married to him and they shared their lives, she finally understands that she never really knew him.

> Shows understanding

At the end of the story, Elizabeth realises that one of the most important roles she plays – being a wife – has suddenly come to an end and she has nothing

to replace it. She also understands that she never loved her husband, indeed that she never really knew him. Throughout her entire marriage she has been living with someone who is effectively a stranger and she only realises this after he has died. As she thinks, 'There had been nothing between them'. There is nothing – not even the child she is expecting – she can look forward to. She has been defeated by life.

> Shows interpretation

The arrival of her husband's body and the ritual of washing it brings Elizabeth to a sad epiphany: she and her husband had been 'two isolated beings'. Even when they were making love ('exchanging their nakedness repeatedly', which might imply that they were equal partners sexually), Lawrence notes that 'There had been nothing between them'. Elizabeth's feeling that nothing in their marriage, even their physicality, had held any meaning, that it was 'utter, intact separateness', gives her a kind of tragic status. She understands that her life has been meaningless and she realises that she must go on. It is no wonder that the baby she is expecting feels 'like ice in her womb'.

> Shows exploration

In her womb was an ice of fear, because of this separate stranger with whom she had been living as one flesh.

> The pit-bank loomed up … flames like red sores licking its ashy sides, in the afternoon's stagnant light.

Analysing structure

The story begins in the late afternoon and there are many references to time. These references help to give the story a sense of **pace** as it moves towards its climax and also perhaps suggest how time moves on for all the characters and will, eventually, result in their own deaths.

1 What specific references to time can you find in the story? How do these references provide the story with a structure?

2 The story begins at dusk and ends at dawn. Consider what meaning this might have.

Which of these following possibilities do you think is the most likely?

a   It shows a movement from living a lie to seeing the truth.
b   It shows the ending of one life and the beginning of another for Elizabeth.
c   It shows that time passes and all things change naturally.
d   It shows a movement from Walter's death to the new child's birth.

Can you think of any other reasons for this structure?

3 Lawrence also uses footsteps as a way of structuring the story. What is the effect on the reader of the following mentions of footsteps?

a   (When Annie comes home) '**Directly, gratefully, came quick young steps to the door.**'
b   (When they are waiting for Walter to come home) '**the footsteps went past the gate, and the children were not flung out of their play-world.**'
c   (When Elizabeth is waiting alone) '**At a quarter to ten there were footsteps. One person!**'
d   (When the miner arrives ahead of the men bringing Walter's body) '**the gate banged back, and there were heavy feet on the steps.**'

Analysing language

It is important to develop your skills to be able to analyse details of the language used by a writer. This will enable you to identify patterns in the use of language, how they interrelate and the possible meanings in these patterns. A physical detail may imply something more than what it literally is.

1 With a partner, look at this paragraph to see how one student has analysed the description of the Bates's cottage:

At the edge of the ribbed level of sidings squat a low cottage, three steps down from the cinder track. A large bony vine clutched at the house, as if to claw down the tiled roof. Round the bricked yard grew a few wintry primroses. Beyond, the long garden sloped down to a bush-covered brook course. There were some twiggy apple trees, winter-crack trees, and ragged cabbages. Beside the path hung dishevelled pink chrysanthemums, like pink cloths hung on bushes.

> Makes it sound very small and unimportant

> Seems to be threatening or engulfing the house: creates sense of danger

> Repeated sound – this time a violent verb; again house under threat

> Uncared for, useless

> Bedraggled, uncared for; adds to impression of decay

2 On a copy of the paragraph, add some of your own comments to these annotations, and add some annotations of your own.

Symbolism

In this story, we can find **symbolism** in Lawrence's use of dark and light and fire and ice.

1 Working with a partner, identify and note down three quotations from the story for each of the following three threads in the story:

a   cold   b   dark   c   light.

2 Write one sentence for each quotation to explain how Lawrence uses these images and what effect this has on the reader.

A large bony vine clutched at the house, as if to claw down the tiled roof.

Learning checkpoint

Use what you have learnt about 'Odour of Chrysanthemums' so far to answer the following questions.

1 Annotate a copy of the last three sentences of the story to explore their meaning. What do you think Lawrence wants the reader to understand from these sentences?

Then, with peace sunk heavy on her heart, she went about making tidy the kitchen. She knew she submitted to life, which was her immediate master. But from death, her ultimate master, she winced with fear and shame.

2 What are your feelings after reading the story? Rank the following words with the most appropriate at the top and the least appropriate at the bottom. Justify your order.

3 Do you think Lawrence wanted to depress or upset his readers by pointing out all the bad things that can happen in life? Or did he want to make them determined to appreciate happiness and live each day to the full? Discuss your ideas in a small group.

GETTING IT INTO WRITING

Now that you have built on your understanding by interpreting and analysing the text of the story, you have the opportunity to develop your thoughts into a written response. Remember: in your examination, you will be asked to write about two stories, but here you will focus on just one.

1 Use your exploration of the story, and the notes you have taken, to write a response of no more than 300 words to the following question:

How does Lawrence present the characters of the mothers in 'Odour of Chrysanthemums'?

Write about:

- how Lawrence presents the two mothers in the story
- how Lawrence uses the mothers to explore the themes of grief and the ways in which unexpected events can completely change people's lives.

When writing your response to this question, remember to:

- include details of how the story develops
- use short quotations to support your ideas
- explore implied meanings (the ideas behind the words)
- identify different **viewpoints**
- give your own personal response.

✓ **Complete this assignment on Cambridge Elevate.**

Structuring your response

Using the work you have already done in this unit as a starting point, write about the two mothers in the story. You should aim to write at least one paragraph about the mothers' feelings for their family and how they express their grief when Walter dies.

It may help if you think of the question as a 'What' and a 'How'.

- The 'What' is the feelings and attitudes in the story, in this case grief and change.
- The 'How' is the writer's way of conveying those things through language and use of language devices.

For the **first** part, you will need to:

- bring together the notes you made earlier to illustrate the feelings of both of the mothers for their family
- illustrate how these feelings change in the course of the story
- examine their relationships with their family in detail – for example how the relationship between Walter and his mother has changed since he was a child or the ways in which Elizabeth tries to protect her two children from the knowledge of their father's death.

For the **second** part, you will need to show how Lawrence uses his craft as a writer through language and symbolism to:

- show the characters' feelings and attitudes
- represent ideas about how people respond to and try to cope with grief
- show the ways in which unexpected events can destroy families.

Improving your response

1 Here are some extracts from students' responses to the question about the characters of the mothers in 'Odour of Chrysanthemums'. Work with a partner to decide which extracts have gone beyond simple comments about the story to a convincing exploration of language or ideas.

It was chrysanthemums when I married him, and chrysanthemums when you were born, and the first time they ever brought him home drunk, he'd got brown chrysanthemums in his button-hole.

The old tears fell in succession as drops from wet leaves; the mother was not weeping, merely her tears flowed.

Student A

Elizabeth Bates tries to look after her two children. She stops her son from playing in the brook and she tells him off for letting his sleeves get dirty when he is playing with his sister. At the end she makes sure that her children will not see their dead father.

Student B

At the very beginning of the story Elizabeth and her father have a conversation about marriage. Her father has decided that he will remarry. Elizabeth obviously does not approve and tells him that she thinks it is too soon after her own mother's death. Her father, however, says that he does not want to sit at his 'own hearth like a stranger'. This is odd because it is exactly what Elizabeth does later in the story.

Student C

Lawrence uses the symbol of the chrysanthemums in a variety of ways. The 'dishevelled' flowers grow outside the house, suggesting the fractured relationships within. Elizabeth tells John that the discarded leaves look 'nasty', however she keeps a few in her waistband where Annie will later admire them. Elizabeth has three distinct memories of the chrysanthemums: when she married, when Annie was born and when Walter was first brought home drunk. In her mind they are associated with events she wishes had never happened: her marriage and

the birth of her first child are bleak memories. Yet perhaps, at one point, Lawrence implies that there might be some hope, for Elizabeth keeps two vases of them in the parlour, possibly in the hope of her life turning for the better. It is only when one vase is knocked over that this hope disappears and all that remains is the smell of despair.

Student D

'Whatever he was, I remember him when he was little, an' I learned to understand him and to make allowances.' In their own ways, both the wife and the mother, as Lawrence repeatedly calls them, remain distanced from Walter. In the mother's case it is not the man that she is mourning (so dramatically she slips into hysteria) but the child. However, she does realise that he has grown to be a highly flawed man. 'Whatever he was' indicates that she does not want to go into details of his failings as a husband and father. She knows that he has failed but is determined that everyone should 'make allowances', in other words not to pass moral judgements on this behaviour. To her, he will always be her beautiful, wayward son.

Student E

Walter's mother remembers her son as being 'a good lad' and says that he was happy and jolly when he was young. She realises that he has changed and now is a useless father, but she keeps her memory of her little boy warm.

Student F

Lawrence shows that Elizabeth feels that her marriage has been utterly unsuccessful. He emphasises her role within the family by regularly referring to her as 'the wife' rather than by name. This makes her seem less of an individual and more of an object. With Walter's death she has a realisation that she never really knew her husband. They had made love and she had borne him two children but she realises that they never really knew each other; that her marriage was a sham. The foetus in her womb is described as being 'like ice'. The simile shows the way in which she now feels nothing for anyone, even the new life within her. In a story with repeated references to fire and heat she has become cold and completely empty.

2 Having thought about these extracts, go back to your own response. What could you do to improve it?

GETTING FURTHER

1 Working with a partner, research what would probably have happened to the Bates family after the death of Walter. Remember that the story is set in 1911.

2 In a small group, decide on six questions you would like to ask D.H. Lawrence about 'Odour of Chrysanthemums'.

   a   Swap your questions with another group.
   b   Answer the six questions you've been given as if you were Lawrence.

3 After a lesson on this short story, a classmate of yours remarks that in their opinion:

- the story is boring, as nothing much happens
- the symbolism is very obvious
- the characters are one-dimensional
- the story is not interesting or well-written.

How would you defend the story against these accusations?

Key terms

simile: an imaginative comparison that uses 'like' or 'as'.

they had met in the dark and had fought in the dark, not knowing whom they met nor whom they fought.

3

My Polish Teacher's Tie

Helen Dunmore

Your progress in this unit:

- explore how Helen Dunmore presents the thoughts and feelings of the characters
- develop your own interpretation of characters, relationships and events
- understand how Dunmore presents themes and ideas
- explore and analyse how Dunmore's use of language and structure affects the reader
- develop your written response skills.

GETTING STARTED - THE STORY AND YOU

1 Have you ever been treated as if you were not part of a group of people you saw every day? How would you react if you were treated in this way? Would you:

a feel angry
b feel hurt
c laugh it off
d stay calm and put it down to people's ignorance?

2 How far do you think you can make judgements about people from what they wear? Discuss your ideas in a small group.

GETTING CLOSER - FOCUS ON DETAILS

The following activities will help you develop your skills from understanding to interpreting. As you work through this unit, you will also progress from exploring to analysing the story. Keep your own notes as you work through the activities. You will use them to bring together your own written response to the story at the end of the unit.

 Listen to an extract from the story on Cambridge Elevate.

What happens in the story?

Helen Dunmore has divided the story into two main sections. The first section is much shorter than the second.

Think about how the different parts of the story relate to each other.

 If you had to divide the story into six sections, where would you start each section?

 What do the beginning and the ending of the story have in common?

STORY ESSENTIALS

Who

Major characters
Carla Carter, canteen worker
Stefan Jeziorny (Steve), Polish teacher
The Head
Valerie Kenward, teacher

Minor characters
Jade, Carla's daughter
Susie Douglas and Mrs Callendar, teachers

When and where

The story is set in the late 20th century in the school Carla works at and at her home.

Sequence of events

- Canteen worker Carla overhears the Head passing on a message from a Polish teacher wanting an English penfriend.
- Carla asks for his address, because she feels a connection with Poland through her Polish mother.
- The Head is surprised because he meant the message to be for teachers.
- Carla writes and receives letters and poetry from the Polish teacher, Stefan.
- He comes over to England and stays with one of the teachers. This teacher finds him odd and difficult, so the visit doesn't look very successful.
- Carla plucks up courage to introduce herself to Stefan. Despite her fear, he is delighted to meet her. They have a connection that is more important than their jobs and outward appearances.

Themes and ideas

- identity
- status
- stereotypes
- society
- immigration
- prejudice
- narrative voice
- belonging
- relationships

ℹ Contexts

'My Polish Teacher's Tie' was published in 2003. As well as short stories, Helen Dunmore also writes novels, poems and children's books.

*I was born in December 1952, in Yorkshire, the second of four children. My father was the eldest of twelve, and this extended family has no doubt had a strong influence on my life, as have my own children. In a large family you hear a great many stories. You also come to understand very early that stories hold quite different meanings for different listeners, and can be recast from many **viewpoints**.*

Understanding the characters

1 Re-read the opening paragraph of the story. What do the facts in this paragraph tell you about Carla as a person doing a job?

2 Use the evidence in the following table to help you understand the statements about the Head.

The Head	
Statement	**Evidence**
His role as Head is important to him.	• The story refers to him always by his title, 'the Head', not by name. • He is first seen in a staff briefing (he sees the staff for ten minutes, once a week). • He is concerned with policy (OFSTED, teacher exchange). • He is associated strongly with paperwork ('as usual he had a pile of papers in front of him', 'wagging the papers', 'wagging a sheaf of papers in front of him', 'bumbled around us flapping his papers').
His language and behaviour in relation to the teaching staff are mainly professional with some attempts to be personal, too.	• After the meeting he 'smiled' and 'raised his eyebrows'; later he beams 'at nobody'. • He is important to the teachers (after the meeting he 'vanished in a knot of teachers wanting to talk to him'). • The teachers need to consult him (Mrs Callendar wants to speak with him about OFSTED). • He turns talking to one teacher into an opportunity for staff communication: 'one minute he's talking to you and the next it's a public announcement'. • He knows and refers to teachers by name ('Mrs Kenward' and then 'Valerie').
His language and behaviour in relation to the catering staff and with the visiting teacher from Poland are less confident and controlled.	• He can't remember Carla's name. • He doesn't know about her personally and is surprised at her request to correspond with the Polish teacher. • Carla is invisible to him and the staff. • He thinks there will be trouble if Carla is approaching him. • He talks to Steve as if he is deaf.

He stitched a nice smile on his face

Now answer these questions:

a The treatment of 'names' is important in this story. The Head is referred to only by his title, and not by name. What does this tell you about him?

b How does the Head treat the teachers in the school?

c How does he treat other people who work in the school?

d How does he treat visitors?

3 What kind of a person is the Head? Arrange the following words in a diamond shape (1-2-3-2-1), with the most appropriate word to describe the Head at the top and the least appropriate at the bottom.

self-centred	xenophobic	arrogant
proud	pompous	nervous
worried	professional	uncaring

What evidence can you find from the story to support your choices?

Where does the story happen?

Think about where the story takes place. Consider how Helen Dunmore makes the **setting** believable.

1 What impression do you get of where the staff meet? Is it a pleasant, casual place where teachers relax, or a formal place where they gather for business and to be given instructions?

2 What makes the teachers seem different from Carla at the tea serving?

3 What details suggest that this is a place where there is a different status among the people who work there?

Themes and ideas

The first section of the story brings out the themes of identity and self-esteem. Identity is the way we think about ourselves in terms of our age, gender, job, intelligence, values, interests and so on. Self-esteem is the way we think about ourselves in terms of our success, happiness, fulfilment and so on.

Carla feels that her job is boring as well as badly paid, and that the teachers do not treat her as an equal. She sees herself as a worker, not a colleague: a second-class person who is there just to serve them.

She feels that her identity is not complete because she has lost contact with her Polish background, and with the language and songs that were part of her childhood.

1 Carla comments on the catering system in the school by saying: '**Visitors pay, too, or it wouldn't be fair. Very keen on fairness, we are, here.**' Part of Carla's sense of her own identity is her great sense of fairness.

a What is there to suggest that she thinks she is unfairly treated, even though the school thinks that it values fairness?

b Why does being a 'colleague' matter to Carla, when she knows Steve will visit the school?

c How fairly do you think Steve is treated when he visits the school?

2 Do you think the school seems a 'fair' place to work? Explain your answer.

3 Do you think it is important for a school to be fair? If so, why?

PUTTING DETAILS TO USE

Now that you have looked at the story more closely, you can use the details you have discovered to build the important skills you will need to explore the key areas of character, setting and ideas.

Exploring the characters, setting, ideas and feelings

1 What evidence can you find in the text to support the following interpretations of Mrs Kenward's character?

a   She enjoys complaining.
b   She is greedy.
c   She does not have much respect for Carla.
d   She likes to be the centre of attention.
e   She is quick to judge other people.
f   She wants to impress the Head.
g   She judges Steve by what she sees and doesn't see what matters.

2 Now write down what you know about Carla. Make a copy of the following table. Note down one important piece of evidence about each part of her life. Then give a brief interpretation of why this is important.

Carla		
	Evidence	**Interpretation of why it is important**
As a child	Her mother wanted her to keep using Polish and sang her songs but her father thought there was no point to this.	In later life she wishes she had kept up the language and feels she has lost part of her identity.
As a parent		
As a worker		
As an individual		

I dish out tea and buns to the teachers twice a day, and I shovel chips on to the kids' trays at dinner-time. It's not a bad job. I like the kids.

3 A student was asked to write about the character of the Head. This is what they wrote:

> *The Head is an important person because all the teachers listen to him when he gives them information and some of them need to talk to him afterwards. He knows some of the staff by their first name but he's not sure of Carla's name. He thinks it's a good idea to have a Polish exchange teacher but he assumes that the people who will be interested are 'colleagues', not non-teaching staff.*

Using this interpretation of the Head as an example, write three sentences in response to each of the following tasks:

a Describe, with supporting evidence from the text, your impressions of Steve/Stefan.

b Describe, with supporting evidence, the school and what sort of place it is.

c Describe some of the strong feelings and attitudes shown by one of the characters.

Learning checkpoint

Identify three pieces of evidence from the text that helped you to form an opinion about one of the following:

- a character
- the setting for the story
- a feeling or attitude.

Write a sentence to explain how each of the quotations supports your interpretation.

The narrator's standpoint

'My Polish Teacher's Tie' is written as a **first-person narrative**. The readers experience the story from Carla's viewpoint. We see what she sees and her thoughts help us to form our own judgements. We trust what she tells us about others and about herself.

In some first-person narratives, the reader cannot rely on the truth of what the narrator tells them. Such characters are called 'unreliable narrators'.

What the characters say and do

1 Helen Dunmore gives us a clear impression of the main character, Carla, in the opening paragraph of the story.

> I wear a uniform, blue overall and white cap with the school logo on it. Part-time catering staff, that's me, £3.89 per hour. I dish out tea and buns to the teachers twice a day, and I shovel chips on to the kids' trays at dinner-time. It's not a bad job. I like the kids.

Annotate a copy of the paragraph to show:

a a personal voice
b suggestions of low self-esteem
c her attitude to her job.

2 Carla says: '**If ever anyone brought up their kids to be pleased with themselves, it's Valerie Kenward.**'

a How might some readers interpret 'being pleased with yourself' in a positive way?
b How might some readers interpret 'being pleased with yourself' in a negative way?

How the characters relate to each other

Writers also use **dialogue** to give readers an understanding of characters and relationships. The way people speak to each other can reveal a lot about themselves and the way they see others.

1 What do the following quotations tell you about the Head's relationship with Carla?

a 'Oh, er – Mrs, er – Carter. Is there a problem?'
b 'I didn't realize you were Polish, Mrs ... er...'

2 Can you identify any other examples of what the Head says that shows something similar about how he relates to Carla?

  **Watch an expert discuss key themes and ideas in the story on Cambridge Elevate.**

How the characters are presented

Helen Dunmore does not present her characters neutrally, by only giving facts about them. She includes details of behaviour and setting to manipulate the reader's feelings about the characters. For example Dunmore tells us that Mrs Kenward:

- complains about the buns
- asks impatiently if the tea is ready yet.

These snapshots of Mrs Kenward's attitude and behaviour do not make the reader respond well to her as a character.

Consider Mrs Kenward's response to the Polish teacher, Steve, who is a guest at her home:

- She rolls her eyes when asked about him.
- She says he is '**hard work**' because he talks about poetry, speaks with an accent and has what she considers to be bad taste in ties.

Working in a pair, write brief notes in answer to the following questions:

1 How does Mrs Kenward's response to Steve as a guest in her home make us feel about her?

2 What do you think about her reasons for finding her role as host '**hard work**'? Write three sentences.

3 How does Mrs Kenward's response make the reader feel about Steve?

4 Can you identify any other details that Dunmore uses to make the reader feel unsympathetic towards Mrs Kenward?

Exploring language and identity

There are several references to language in the story, for example the songs Carla sang with her mother. Language is an important part of a person's identity, as well as part of their culture and heritage. It is a sign to others (like a special tie) that shows you belong to a group.

Helen Dunmore uses Steve's two poems to develop the themes of identity and self-expression. The poems suggest to the reader that a personal voice and language are important parts of an individual's identity.

The second poem Steve sends Carla is about her, and about '**being half-Polish and half-English**'. It contains these lines:

'Mother, I've lost the words you gave me.
Call the police, tell them
there's a reward, I'll do anything ...'

It suggests that there is something valuable about language that has been lost and that it is a pity to lose it.

1 Explore how important language seems to Carla. Why does she ask Steve to send her a copy of the first poem in Polish, although his letters are in English? Does she want to learn some Polish again or is there another reason?

2 Explore the impression you get of Steve from the letters between him and Carla. Create a mind map of your ideas. For example:

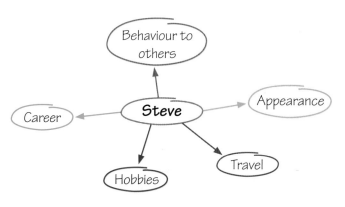

3 What evidence is there in the text that Carla feels 'invisible' to some of the teachers?

4 Do you think the other teachers, or the Head, would be interested in what Carla might have to say? Explain your answer.

5 Which of the following statements do you feel best describes Steve's first poem, and why?

a   It is a sad poem about the death of a bird in a coal mine.

b   It is a **metaphor** for Carla herself: she has sung but the part of her that was Polish has died.

c   It is Steve's own way of expressing his own ideas and feelings.

d   It is Steve's attempt to be something more than a schoolteacher.

6 The following examples of students' work show how you can develop your **understanding** into **interpretation** to **explore** other possible meanings. What differences do you notice in the three answers, in response to the following question:

How does Dunmore present Steve and his relationship with Carla?

He likes poetry and he is interested in Carla's life. ⟵ Shows understanding

He sympathises with Carla's feelings about losing her Polish language and tries to make her feel better about it. He is a caring man who wants to set up a school magazine and he asks her permission to use the poem about her. ⟵ Shows interpretation

Shows exploration

He may be quite lonely as he has asked for an English penfriend, or he may want a chance to improve his English. When Dunmore describes him, he's nervous and sweaty and not confident in a new environment, so that suggests he is not a confident person. Dunmore may be showing that he and Carla are similar not just because of the Polish background, but because they don't fit in with their environment.

Key terms

metaphor: an imaginative comparison in which one thing is said to be another.

This bird flew down the main shaft and got lost in the tunnels underground, then it sang and sang until it died. Everyone heard it singing, but no one could find it.

Analysing language, form and structure

Writers choose their words in both narrative and speech to convey a range of ideas, feelings and attitudes. Even a short, simple sentence can show how a writer has chosen words carefully, to suggest – or **imply** – meaning.

Remember that what a character **says** may not always be what they **mean**.

1 What are the possible implied meanings in Mrs Kenward's statement: '**Isn't that tea made yet?**' Rank the following statements according to which you think is the best interpretation, down to which is least appropriate. Explain your decisions.

    a   She is in a rush.
    b   She is very thirsty.
    c   She thinks she is so important that her tea should be ready whenever she wants it.
    d   She is annoyed that the tea is not ready.
    e   She thinks making tea is a menial job.

2 Carla says: '**It's not a bad job. I like the kids.**' What do you think this comment suggests about her attitude to other aspects of the job?

3 Carla comments that when she approaches the Head, he '**stitched a nice smile on his face**'. Which of the following statements do you think comes nearest to the implied meaning of Carla's comment? Explain your answer.

    a   He smiles nicely.
    b   He wants people to feel at ease so he smiles to show he's friendly.
    c   He forces a smile as his smile doesn't always come naturally.
    d   He thinks that if he smiles people won't question his decisions.
    e   He thinks he is much more important than anyone else but doesn't want them to know this.

Facts and impressions

Language is often used to provide facts or an accurate description, for example Carla's white cap with the school logo on it in the first paragraph of the story. At other times it may be used to create an impression with an implied meaning, and the reader is left to decide what the meaning is.

Sometimes a writer packs a lot of meaning into a very short phrase, such as when Helen Dunmore writes that Steve's choice of tie is '**terribly hopeful**'. This is an unusual choice of words to describe a tie, so Dunmore must have had a very good reason for using them.

 On a copy of the following extract, highlight any details that are purely **factual** in blue and any details that create an **impression** in yellow. For example:

> He was wearing a brown suit with padded shoulders. It looked too big for him. His tie was wider than normal ties, and it was red with bold green squiggles on it. It was a terribly hopeful tie. His shoes had a fantastic shine on them. His face looked much too open, much too alive, as if a child Jade's age had got into an adult's body.

 What do you think makes Steve's choice of tie '**hopeful**'?

3 Why do you think the author describes the tie as not just hopeful, but '**terribly**' hopeful?

Symbolism

Sometimes, a physical detail represents something more than what it literally is. For example a flag is a symbol of nationality, but can also symbolise support or conquest.

The tie is an important symbol in this story. It is a way of representing the themes of identity and judgement based on appearance. The tie is used to show something about the attitude of Mrs Kenward and something about the personality of Steve. The story ends with Carla saying to Steve that she likes his tie.

There is also **symbolism** in Steve's poem, with the image of the bird singing in the mine, representing a person struggling to make themselves heard in a hostile environment.

1 Work with a partner to discuss the following quotations about clothing. Think about:

   a   how clothing may be related to status
   b   how clothing may reveal attitudes based on fashion, dress sense or simple prejudice.

I wear a uniform, blue overall and white cap with the school logo on it.

He was wearing a brown suit with padded shoulders … His tie was wider than normal ties, and it was red with bold green squiggles on it.

his big bright tie blazing

His red tie with bold green squiggles was much too wide and much too bright. It was a flag from another country, a better country than the ones either of us lived in. 'I like your tie,' I said.

> He stood there holding on to my hand right in the middle of the staffroom, his big bright tie blazing

A Polish song. I knew it, I knew it.

Exploring a key moment in the story

The moment Carla and Steve sing together in the staffroom is a key point in the story. The two of them are not ashamed or embarrassed to be singing a duet, in Polish, in an English school. The singing bonds them in an environment in which they both feel uncomfortable.

1 In what ways do you think the song Carla and Steve sing is significant? Working in a small group, rank these statements in order of how appropriate they are as interpretations of the song. Discuss the reasons for your ranking:

  a   Carla can remember a Polish song her mother taught her.
  b   They both enjoy singing.
  c   Carla is proud of her Polish heritage.
  d   People from two countries have done something wonderful together.
  e   Carla is now a complete person: part English and part Polish.

2 How has the structure of the story led up to this moment? You might like to consider threads about:

  a   speaking Polish
  b   self-esteem
  c   identity
  d   being invisible or highly visible in the staffroom
  e   the instinctive connections between Carla and Steve, which hold a hope of something better.

3 Here are some alternative titles for 'My Polish Teacher's Tie'. Rank them in order of suitability and explain your choices.

  a   'The Songs My Mother Taught Me'
  b   'A Caged Bird in a Coal Mine'
  c   'Polish Letters'
  d   'Another Country's Flag'
  e   'Ties'.

Learning checkpoint

Helen Dunmore has created a character who is a bit of an outsider in her workplace. When she asks for the address of the Polish teacher so that she can write to him, the Head is surprised, thinking the request was directed to a teacher, not a canteen assistant. When the Polish teacher comes to the school, Carla feels awkward and afraid that he will be disappointed to find that she is not a teacher. However, he is glad to meet her and more comfortable with her than with the teachers.

1 Write a short paragraph in response to each of the following questions:

a Why do you think Carla asked for the Polish teacher's address in the first place?

b Why did she think of ways to avoid coming to work when she knew he was coming?

c How did she feel when he sang?

d What lessons do you think Carla could give the teachers about life?

GETTING IT INTO WRITING

Throughout this unit you have built on your understanding by interpreting and analysing. You will now have the opportunity to develop your thoughts into a written response. In your examination, you will be asked to write about two stories, but here you will focus on just one.

1 Use your exploration of the story, and the notes you have taken, to write a response of no more than 300 words to the following question:

> How does Dunmore present the character of Carla in 'My Polish Teacher's Tie'?
>
> Write about:
>
> • how Dunmore presents Carla's feelings and attitudes
> • how Dunmore uses Carla to explore the themes of identity and self-esteem.

✓ **Complete this assignment on Cambridge Elevate.**

Structuring your response

Remember the 'What' and the 'How':

• The 'What' is the sequence of events and the 'feelings and attitudes' (such as self-esteem and identity).
• The 'How' is the writer's way of conveying those things through language and language devices.

To answer the **first** part of the question, you can bring together the notes you made earlier in this unit. These will help you to illustrate the feelings of Carla and her attitudes to herself and those around her, including her mother and her daughter, as well as the teachers and Steve.

To answer the **second** part of the question, you will need to show how Dunmore uses language to make readers see what causes Carla's low self-esteem and how it affects her. You will also need to show how she suggests that self-esteem can be rebuilt by seeing identity as more than a job or a uniform.

For both parts of the question you should show how Dunmore's craft as a writer involves using language and symbolism to show feelings and attitudes, and to represent ideas about human needs and human qualities, for example in what the characters say, the image of the bird in the mine and Steve's tie.

Improving your response

1 Here are some extracts from students' responses to the question about the character of Carla in 'My Polish Teacher's Tie'. Work with a partner to decide which extracts have gone beyond simple comments about the story to a convincing exploration of language or ideas.

Student A

Dunmore creates a character who is caught between two cultures and feels that something is missing from her life. The bird in the coal mine is a metaphor for Carla's situation: she too is lost because she can no longer sing the songs her mother taught her and, like the bird, something inside her has died. She can't find self-esteem in her job and she feels her identity is not complete because she has lost her Polish songs and language. Dunmore uses the Polish teacher's tie as a symbol of appearances that can lead to false judgements about a person. Some may see the tie as a sign of inferiority or poor taste, but she sees it as an emblem of 'a better country than the ones either of us lived in', where trivial things like dress are less important than more valuable human qualities of sympathy, understanding and respect.

Student B

Carla is always very aware of what is going on around her. She may be invisible to the teachers (she observes that they 'are used to getting out of the way of catering staff without really seeing them') but she knows about the Head's attempts to be liked by smiling but all he can do is 'bumble' in a useless manner and Mrs Kenward's greed and snobbery. For Carla, the teachers she serves with tea and buns are a pretty sorry lot, pretending to believe in fairness but always ready to moan about stale buns and sneer at people who are different. She can rise above Mrs Kenward's nasty put-down of Steve and say she likes his tie because Steve has shown her understanding and respect.

It was a flag from another country, a better country than the ones either of us lived in.

Student C

Carla enjoys writing to Steve. She adds to her letter each day and imagines that she is talking to him. That is why she uses his name in the letters. However, she doesn't tell him that she is not a teacher. She says 'Let him think what he wanted to think. I wasn't lying'. But she wasn't telling the strict truth either and that is why she is so worried later in the story.

Student D

Carla seems to be a good mother to Jade. She offers her the Polish stamp and drives her to tea at a friend's house. She even decides not to throw away the book of poetry because it might come in useful for Jade. There is no mention of Jade's father so Jade is the only family Carla now has. Her care for her daughter is in contrast to Mrs Kenward and Philippa who, according to Carla, has been brought up to be pleased with herself. This helps to show Carla is a loving mother. Also, unlike Mrs Kenward, she does not judge people by the clothes they wear, like Steve's tie.

Student E

Carla works at a school as a part-time catering assistant. Her mother was Polish but Carla cannot remember any Polish songs. She writes letters to Steve who is a Polish teacher. Steve visits her school. In the staffroom they sing a Polish song. Carla remembers the words and is happy.

Student F

Helen Dunmore creates a very realistic voice for Carla. In the first paragraph the reader learns that she is forced to wear a uniform in school, which puts her on the same level as the pupils. Her cap even has a logo on it as if she were some sort of brand. Dunmore also creates sympathy for Carla by conveying her low self-esteem because of how poorly she is paid, and how she is overlooked by the teachers. Dunmore shows that Carla has a very demotivated attitude to her job: she has to 'dish out tea' and 'shovel chips': both verbs show that she does not really take her job seriously. It is interesting that she says 'I like the kids'. The implication is that she does not like the teachers.

2 Having thought about these extracts, go back to your own response. What could you do to improve it?

GETTING FURTHER

1 In a small group, discuss possible reasons for Dunmore's choice of title for her short story.

2 Look again at the story. Imagine you were to cut out all the narrative and leave just the dialogue.

   a Would the dialogue alone make a good playscript? What would be lost?
   b Try thinking about it the other way: would the narrative alone make a good story? What would be lost?
   c As a group, decide which would be the better reduced version.

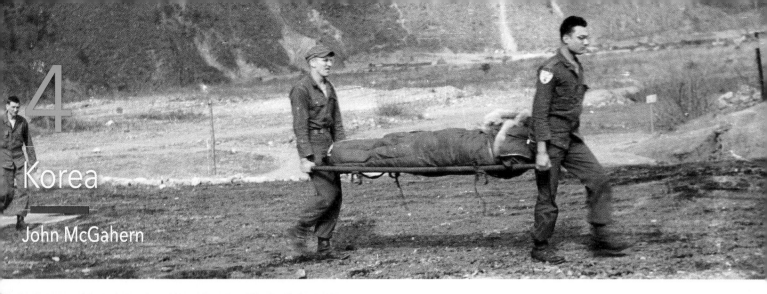

4

Korea

John McGahern

Your progress in this unit:

- explore how John McGahern presents the thoughts and feelings of the characters
- develop your own interpretation of characters, relationships and events
- understand how McGahern presents themes and ideas
- explore and analyse how McGahern's use of language and structure affects the reader
- develop your written response skills.

GETTING STARTED – THE STORY AND YOU

1 Imagine you overheard two people talking about you on the other side of a door. What would you do? Would you:

  a cough loudly and go through the door
  b turn around and go away
  c stay quiet and listen carefully to what they were saying?

If you chose the last option, what would you then do if:

  a the people were saying good things about you
  b the people were saying bad things about you?

2 Have you ever posted a bad comment about someone on social media? Has someone ever done it to you? How did it make you feel?

3 In order to understand this short story, it is helpful to know something of the **context**. In a small group, research some basic facts about **either** the Irish War of Independence (1919–22) **or** the Korean War (1950–53). Share your findings with the rest of the class.

Key terms

context: the historical circumstances of a piece of writing, which affect what an author wrote and why they wrote it.

'You saw an execution then too, didn't you?' I asked my father, and he started to tell as he rowed.

STORY ESSENTIALS

Who

Main characters
A father
A son

Minor characters
Farrell, a cattle dealer
Moran, a neighbour
Luke Moran, his dead son

When and where

The events in the story take place at some point during the Korean War (1950–53) in Oakport, a fictional town in rural Ireland.

Sequence of events

- A young man and his father are fishing in a rowing boat. The father tells the son about an execution he witnessed during the Irish War of Independence.
- They then discuss the son's future: he has just taken his school Leaving Certificate. His father suggests that he goes to America, the land of opportunity.
- Later in the same day, the son overhears his father talking to a cattle dealer about a local boy who went to America and was then called up to fight in the Korean War. He was killed and his father received a lot of money, which has changed his life.
- The father and son go fishing in the evening and the father again asks about the possibility of the son going to America. The son says he has decided not to go and the story ends in silence.

Themes and ideas

- death
- honour
- migration
- deceit
- becoming an adult
- secrets
- narrative voice
- the end of a way of life
- how the past affects the present

Contexts

John McGahern (1934–2006) was born in Dublin and is considered one of Ireland's most important 20th-century novelists. He wrote 'Korea' in 1970.

I'm only interested in what I know and care about. One of the more uncomfortable facts about growing old is that while you are failing, everything around becomes more interesting, because you know more. One of the hard things about being young is that most of the time you don't know what the hell is going on around you.

GETTING CLOSER – FOCUS ON DETAILS

The following activities will help you develop your skills from understanding to interpreting. As you work through this unit, you will also progress from exploring to analysing the story. Keep your own notes as you work through the activities. You will use them to bring together your own written response to the story at the end of the unit.

What happens in the story?

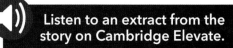

Listen to an extract from the story on Cambridge Elevate.

We understand the story through the eyes of a young man who is relating what happened some years later. This is the same **viewpoint** that is used in both 'Chemistry' and 'A Family Supper' (see Unit 5). So it is a **first-person narrative**, written from the perspective of an adult looking back to a significant moment in his life.

Start with the facts. The story begins with an account of an execution at Mountjoy Prison in Dublin during the Irish War of Independence. The narrator is remembering what his father told him.

1 If you were making a short film of 'Korea', how many scenes would you need? Make a table to note briefly what would happen in each scene and provide a quotation from the story for each. For example:

Scene	What happens in the scene	Quotation
1	In a boat on the river. The father tells his story about the execution he witnessed.	'the boy tore at his tunic over the heart, as if to pluck out the bullets, and the buttons of the tunic began to fly into the air'

2 Note down any references you can find later in the story to:

a the execution in particular
b the Irish War of Independence as a whole.

3 What does the reader learn about the Korean War in the story?

Understanding the characters

1 What impression of the father do you get in the description of his honeymoon? **Annotate** a copy of this paragraph to show how the language is used to describe his feelings and attitudes.

'We sat on top in the open on the wooden seats with the rail around that made it like a small ship. The sea was below, and the smell of the sea and furze-bloom all about, and then I looked down and saw the furze pods bursting, and the way they burst in all directions seemed shocking like the buttons when he started to tear at his tunic. I couldn't get it out of my mind all day. It destroyed the day.'

---

2 What kind of person is the father? Arrange the following words in a diamond shape (1-2-3-2-1) with the most appropriate at the top and the least appropriate at the bottom.

self-centred	proud	callous
ambitious	unfulfilled	desperate
brave	morose	skilled

What evidence can you find to support your choices?

Where does the story happen?

1 Consider how John McGahern creates the **setting** for the reader, and how he makes it interesting and believable. Make notes on the following questions:

a What details make the river in the morning seem peaceful?

b What impression do you have of the river later in the day?

c What details are given of the lavatory?

d What effect do these details have on the reader?

Themes and ideas

The first section of the story is a narrative describing the execution. The father must have mentioned it to someone in the past because the son begins the narrative with a question about the incident. It is the only time when the father discusses the War of Independence with his son. The narrative brings out themes such as:

- bravery
- acceptance of fate
- the arbitrary nature of death in wartime
- the differences between young and old.

1 Re-read the first section of the story, up to the part where the father starts to describe his honeymoon. Then write brief answers to the following questions:

a Why are the two men executed?

b How have they been chosen?

c What details are given of the younger man?

d How does he behave during the execution?

e What details are given of the older man?

f How does he behave during the execution?

g Why does the officer pump five bullets into the older man?

h How do you as a reader react to the description of the execution?

> I looked down and saw the furze pods bursting, and the way they burst in all directions seemed shocking like the buttons when he started to tear at his tunic.

2 Working with a partner, place the following statements in order of importance:

a   The execution shows that people face death in different ways.
b   The execution shows that people should be proud to die for their cause.
c   The execution shows that in wartime there is no reason why some people live and some people die.
d   The execution shows that the winning side is always ruthless.
e   The execution shows that the officer is intent on a revenge that is completely meaningless.

3 Compare your chosen order with another pair. As a group, discuss the importance of the execution in the story.

PUTTING DETAILS TO USE

Now that you have looked at the story more closely, you can use the details you have discovered to build the important skills you will need to explore the key areas of character, setting and ideas.

Exploring the characters, setting, ideas and feelings

1 Explore the father's attitudes and feelings throughout the story by making a table like the following one. Decide which statements are true and which are false, and find evidence in the story to support your decisions.

Statement	True/False	Evidence
The father is worried that his way of making a living is threatened.		
He is haunted by the execution.		
He wants what is best for his son.		
He wants his son to fight (and even die) so he will make some money.		
He has had a miserable and disappointing life.		
He is a romantic who remembers his honeymoon with affection.		
He is used to a hard way of life.		
He is a man much given to silences who finds communication difficult.		
He wants to have authority over his son.		
He wants to live honourably but realises that he has not.		

Before, if I asked him about the war, he'd draw fingers across his eyes as if to tear a spider web away

2 A student was asked to write about the character of the older man in the narrative of the execution. This is what they wrote:

The older man seems to take his impending death with considerable calm, keeping his hands in his pockets and 'chewing very slowly' as if he were in some way mocking the ways in which death comes to those men who fight. His reply to the officer, 'It's a bit too late now in the day for that' is nonchalant, almost sarcastic, and shows that he has no fear. The fact that he falls backwards is put down to his hands being in his pockets: a cynical act of defiance.

Using this interpretation of the older man as an example, write three sentences in response to each of the following tasks.

a   Describe, with supporting details, what the younger man is like.

b   Describe, with supporting details, the river.

c   Describe some of the strong feelings and attitudes shown by the characters.

The narrator's standpoint

'Korea' is written as a first-person narrative. As in 'Chemistry', the reader is given a narrative account of a series of events from the point of view of someone who was young at the time and has now grown up and is looking back on the events they are describing.

This means that they have an adult's perspective on the characters, including themselves, and the reader trusts their perceptions and judgements. They are, we can assume, reliable narrators. What they say happened, really did happen; what they say they felt, they did feel.

What the characters say and do

In the character of the father, John McGahern creates a man who might be considered to be a monster – a little like the father in 'A Family Supper' (see Unit 5).

Learning checkpoint

Select three pieces of evidence from the text that helped you to form an opinion of one of the following:

- a character
- the setting for the story
- a feeling or attitude.

Write a sentence to explain how each of the quotations supports your interpretation.

1 Working with a partner, look again at the character of the father and try to find evidence for the five statements in the table:

The father	
Statement	Evidence
He is very frustrated because he thinks he should have a position of importance in the community but he is only a poor farmer and fisherman.	
He feels that fighting in the War of Independence was a waste of his time.	
He feels that he is being pushed out by the tourists who will only fish for pleasure.	
He is jealous of Moran because he has suddenly become an important and wealthy man in the community.	
He is willing to sacrifice the life of his son in order to better himself.	

2 Now rank the statements in order of how well they describe the character of the father, giving your reasons for your decisions. Then answer the following questions.

a Can you understand why the father thinks as he does?
b What do you think about his relationship with his son?
c How do you react to the father?

How the characters are presented

John McGahern does not present characters in a straightforward way. He does provide some detail of what the characters do, but he does not give the reader any physical description of them. This means the reader has to create their own image of the characters' appearance.

You have already seen that in some stories in *Telling Tales* what is **said** is not always what is **meant**. There are also moments of silence when what is **not** said is just as important. You may be able to relate this to your own experience. There may well have been occasions when you decided to say nothing. This may have been to hide your feelings of, for example, embarrassment, shame or anger. Perhaps you may not have understood what has been said, and you did not want to appear foolish.

'It'll be my own funeral,' I answered

1 Consider these moments of silence in the story:

'Sounds a bit highfalutin' to me. Comes from going to school too long,' he said aggressively, and I was silent.

'It'll be my own funeral,' I answered, and asked after a long silence, 'As you grow older, do you find your own days in the war and jails coming much back to you?'

I knew this silence was fixed for ever as I rowed in silence till he asked, 'Do you think, will it be much good tonight?'

    a   What do you imagine the characters are thinking?
    b   What other references to silence can you find in the story?
    c   Why do you think McGahern has included them?

2 The unnamed narrator, the son, is important in this story.

    a   Working with a partner, select five facts about the narrator.
    b   What do you think these facts tell the reader about the narrator?

3 The following examples of students' work show how you can develop your **understanding** into **interpretation** to **explore** other possible meanings. What differences do you notice in the three answers, in response to the following question?

How does McGahern present the character of the narrator?

The narrator has just finished his Leaving Certificate exams but does not know how he has done. He will either go on to further study or he will look for a job. What seems certain is that he will no longer help his father with the fishing. ⟵ Shows understanding

The narrator feels that he is standing between childhood and adulthood. His school days are over and his adult days are about to start. His father appears to realise this as well, for McGahern writes that he wanted 'to give of himself before it ended'. It is not just the narrator's childhood that will end. The father's way of life is also threatened, but it is only later that the narrator comes to realise that his own death may be the way to solve his father's problems.

> Shows interpretation

McGahern's narrator looks back on the incidents of that day on the river and later when he is in the lavatory with a considerable amount of objectivity. The narrator is well aware that his childhood had ended with his final exams and that he will move away from his father geographically and emotionally. He hopes that he will have 'choices' but is also prepared to put up with what he can get. When he overhears his father discussing Luke Moran with Farrell he realises what his father wishes for him and why he suggested going to America. He describes 'the shock' and the realisation that 'my youth had ended' just as the life of the young soldier had ended in Mountjoy. He remembers with affection the time father and son were bonded in the excitement of the Final, with the father providing the adult, masculine support for the young son, but realises that, however close he felt at that moment, this bond has gone forever. He knows that 'I was discarding his life to assume my own' as the old order must always be replaced by the young.

> Shows exploration

Exploring themes and ideas

1 Working with a partner, note down all the references to Ireland in the story.

a What impression do these descriptions create?
b What are the pressures that face the father?
c What do you think he means when he says towards the end of the story: **'if I'd conducted my own wars, and let the fool of a country fend for itself, I'd be much better off today'**?

2 In his memoir, John McGahern wrote: *'We grow into an understanding of the world gradually. Much of what we come to know is far from comforting.'*

To what extent do you think this is a fair description of what happens to the narrator in 'Korea'?

The shock I felt was the shock I was to feel later when I made some social blunder, the splintering of a self-esteem

3 Four students were asked what they thought was the most important theme of 'Korea'. They replied:

> It's about the ways in which young people grow up and move on, leaving old people behind them.

> It's about the end of a simple, rural way of life and a man who cannot accept that his own importance is diminished.

> It's about how a father is prepared to help his own son be killed so that he can claim the insurance money and have a better life.

> It's about the ways youth and innocence die and are often murdered by forces that are inherently evil and all-powerful.

    a   Working with a partner, what evidence do you think these four students could give to support their ideas?

    b   What do you think the main theme(s) of the story are?

4 In what way is the title of the story a **pun**?

Analysing language, form and structure

1 Compare the beginning and end of the story:

    a   Who is rowing and who is fishing?

    b   Who is asking questions?

    c   How is the execution at Mountjoy presented in different ways?

    d   How has the balance of power been changed?

2 Why do you think McGahern included such detailed descriptions of the process of fishing in the river?

3 A student annotated the description of the river in this way:

> People hadn't woken yet, and the early morning cold and mist were on the river. Outside of the slow ripple of the oars and the threshing of the fish on the line beaded with running drops of water as it came in, the river was dead silent, except for the occasional lowing of cattle on the banks.

Alone, cut off from world, private

Emphasises they are alone – cannot see or be seen

Contrast to slow regularity (rural Ireland?)

Another reference to silence: what is not said is as important as what is said. Middle of the sentence.

Irony – the cows are talking to each other but the people aren't

a Develop or adapt some of these annotations and then add two of your own.

b How do you think this paragraph contributes to the **atmosphere** of the story?

4 Re-read the description of Luke Moran's funeral (starting 'Luke Moran's body had come from Korea in a leaden casket') and annotate a copy of these lines.

Exploring a key moment in the story

A key moment in this story is when the narrator realises what his father will do to try to re-establish his place as an important figure in the community. He is prepared to send his son to fight for the USA in a civil war on the far side of the world and should his son be killed, then this would be a welcome financial bonus. Two hundred and fifty dollars a month would be good; ten thousand dollars for a death would be better, especially with the added attraction of a military funeral.

1 Re-read the section of the story that recounts the conversation between the father and Farrell (starting 'I saw him stretch across the wall in conversation with the cattle-dealer Farrell'). Then answer the following questions:

a How does the narrator imply that local people were impressed by Luke Moran's funeral?

b Why do you think the father was excited when he spoke to Farrell?

c Why does McGahern place the narrator in such an unpleasant setting?

d How does he emphasise this unpleasantness?

e Looking back on this moment, the narrator explains it as similar to making a social blunder. What do you think he means by the phrase 'the splintering of a self-esteem'?

Key terms

pun: a 'play on words' – the use of a word with a double meaning. A pun may have the same spelling but different meanings or different spellings (and different meanings) but sound alike.

irony: the use of words to imply the opposite of, or something different from, what is said.

the river was dead silent, except for the occasional lowing of cattle on the banks.

each month he'd get so many dollars while I served, and he'd get ten thousand if I was killed.

 Learning checkpoint

In the character of the father, McGahern has created a man who has a sense of failure. He is about to lose his fishing licence so that foreign tourists can fish the river in his place and he will not be able to survive on the potato crop alone. He fought for an independent Ireland; he might have died for it, but the random nature of the reprisal executions saved him. His son is leaving him to pursue his own life.

1 Write brief notes in answer to the following questions:

a Why do you think he decides to tell his son about the Mountjoy executions?

b Why does he say: '**There's no room for ambition in this poky place.**'?

c What does he think about his country?

d What does he think about his son?

e What does he think about himself?

GETTING IT INTO WRITING

As you have worked through this unit, you have built on your understanding by analysing and interpreting the text. You will now have the opportunity to develop your ideas into a written response.

1 Use your exploration of the story, and the notes you have taken, to write a response to the following question:

How does John McGahern present the father in 'Korea'?

Write about:

- how McGahern presents the father's feelings and attitudes
- how McGahern uses the father to present the themes of honour and deceit.

✓ **Complete this assignment on Cambridge Elevate.**

Structuring your response

Remember the 'What' and the 'How' – **what** the story is about and **how** is it written.

- The 'What' is the 'feelings and attitudes' of the father.
- The 'How' is the writer's way of conveying the character through language and language devices.

For the **first** part, you will need to bring together the notes you made earlier about the father. These will help you to get started. Remember that you are exploring:

- how the father behaves during the story
- how he responds to his son
- how he responds to the world around him.

You could also explore:

- how the father was affected by his experience in wartime
- how he views people who he thinks have behaved in an honourable way (the Mountjoy executions).

For the **second** part, you will need to write about the ways in which McGahern has used language and structure in 'Korea'.

You could consider:

- the importance of language in the story (How does the father express himself to his son? How does the son describe his father?)
- the ways in which the writer suggests that the father is unhappy and feels that his way of life is being threatened by forces beyond his control
- the ways in which McGahern uses silence
- the ways in which the son comments on his father's actions and attitudes when narrating the stories.

> Each move he made I watched as closely as if I too had to prepare myself to murder.

Improving your response

1 Here are some extracts from students' responses to the question about the father. Work with a partner to decide which extracts have gone beyond simple comments about the story to a convincing exploration of language or ideas.

Student A

John McGahern creates a frustrated character in the father who seems to feel as though he has failed. His memories of the war and the death of the young soldier have stayed with him and he remembers the young man's buttons on his honeymoon. He declares: 'I couldn't get it out of my mind all day. It destroyed the day.' The repetition of the word 'day' implies that it is not just the honeymoon that was spoilt, but all the days of his life. He has failed to win his personal war for independence and has become a poor fisherman and farmer. His son represents his one chance of success.

Student B

The father is very poor. He is the last man to fish on the river and he also grows potatoes. His son has now finished school and his father wants him to go to America so that he can be called up and sent to Korea to fight in the war. He will be well paid for this and so can send money back to his father. It seems that his father would not mind very much if he were killed so that he can have the insurance money, which will make him a very rich man in rural Ireland.

Student C

The father wants his son to go to America so that he can fight in the Korean War and earn 250 dollars a month. If the son gets killed the father will receive 10,000 dollars just like Luke Moran's father did.

Student D

McGahern positions the father in between the two executed soldiers. One was blindfolded; the other met his death with eyes wide open. The father, when he speaks of the war draws his fingers across his eyes 'as if to tear a spider web away'. The **simile** indicates that he has partial vision: he is neither young hero nor old cynic. His vision of the world around him is obscured in some way, perhaps due to his bitterness. The son then notes that his father seemed to 'want to talk, to give of himself before it ended'. This unexpected communication elevates the son to the status of an adult and marks the ending of his childhood in the same way as the Leaving Certificate marks his opportunity to become independent.

Student E

The father asks his son a number of questions about his future. The boy says that these will depend upon his exam results: 'there's no use counting chickens, is there?' The father is then described as being 'calculating' which means that he is thinking about his next question and how the conversation should develop. The father then asks if the boy has considered 'throwing this country up altogether and going to America'. These words are 'fumbled for' as if the father does not want his son to know why he is asking the questions.

Student F

The father discusses the Korean War with Farrell. His son overhears the conversation, which is about Luke Moran who has been killed in Korea. Luke's father has received 10,000 dollars and is 'buying cattle left and right' because he has now become a rich man. The father also wants to be rich.

2 Having thought about these extracts, go back to your own response. What could you do to improve it?

GETTING FURTHER

1 A eulogy is a speech or piece of writing in praise of someone who has recently died (or something that has recently ended). In some ways, 'Korea' is a eulogy for the traditional way of life in rural Ireland, which was dying.

Working with a partner, write a short eulogy that the son might have delivered for his father at his funeral.

2 This picture is from the 1995 film *Korea*.

Choose any of the conversations in the story and **storyboard** them for a film version. You should try to include a variety of shots (close-ups, medium and long shots, tracking and panning) to make the film visually interesting. You also need to provide the **dialogue** in the form of captions.

5

A Family Supper

Kazuo Ishiguro

Your progress in this unit:

- explore how Kazuo Ishiguro presents the thoughts and feelings of the characters
- develop your own interpretation of characters, relationships and events
- understand how Ishiguro presents themes and ideas
- explore and analyse how Ishiguro's use of language and structure affects the reader
- develop your written response skills.

GETTING STARTED – THE STORY AND YOU

1. Look at these images linked to the story. They are associated with Japanese traditions. Do some research to find out about each one.

2. What traditions do you associate with your culture?

Japanese tea room

Samurai

Fugu

STORY ESSENTIALS

Who

Main characters
The narrator, a young man
His father
Kikuko, the narrator's younger sister

Minor characters
The narrator's mother, who died from poison
Mr Watanabe, who committed suicide after killing his wife and his two little girls
Suichi, Kikuko's boyfriend
Vicki, the narrator's ex-girlfriend

When and where

The story is set at the family house in Kamakura, a coastal city in Japan, in the late 20th century.

Sequence of events

- A young man returns to the family home in Kamakura, Japan, after living in California for a number of years.
- He discovers that his mother's death, two years before, was caused by eating fugu, a fish that can be poisonous.
- The father's business has collapsed and he tells the son that his business partner, Mr Watanabe, killed his own family and committed suicide out of shame.
- Father and son have a strained conversation with many silences.
- Kikuko, his lively student sister, arrives. Sister and brother go into the garden where they discuss her future plans, their mother and the narrator's memory of seeing a ghost in the garden.
- They then return to the house to eat. The father has cooked fish.
- The story ends with the son admitting that he does not know if he will return to America or stay with his father.

Themes and ideas

- identity
- honour
- youth and age
- maternal love
- guilt
- forgiveness
- narrative voice
- belonging
- relationships

Contexts

Kazuo Ishiguro was born in Nagasaki in 1954 but left Japan as a young child when his family moved to the UK in 1960. His 1989 novel *The Remains of the Day* won the Man Booker Prize and was turned into a film that was nominated for eight Oscars. He wrote 'A Family Supper' in 1982.

Perhaps I expect too much of a reader. I seem to assume that people are going to go through my books very carefully. You have to make a choice somewhere. You have either to address the reader who is going to be reading carefully or address the person who isn't. If you spell everything out or broadcast everything it's frustrating for the person who is reading it carefully.

GETTING CLOSER – FOCUS ON DETAILS

The following activities will help you develop your skills from understanding to interpreting. As you work through this unit, you will also progress from exploring to analysing the story. Keep your own notes as you work through the activities. You will use them to bring together your own written response to the story at the end of the unit.

 Listen to an extract from the story on Cambridge Elevate.

What happens in the story?

There are five main conversations in the story. These take place between:

- father and son in the tea-room
- brother and sister in the garden
- father and son during a tour of the house
- father and son over dinner
- father and son in the tea-room.

1 Working in a small group, choose four quotations for each conversation that sum up what is happening.

    a Practise saying these speeches out loud in a small group.

    b Act out your choices for other groups.

Understanding the characters

1 Look at the evidence in the following table to help you understand the statements about the narrator's father. Then answer the questions.

    a What does the son's description of his father tell the reader about the father's character?

    b How does the father treat his children?

    c What does he think about Mr Watanabe?

    d What does he think of the modern world?

    e What does he imply by saying to his son, '**I don't suppose you believe in war.**'?

The father	
Statements	**Evidence**
The father appears to be a hard man.	• He looks 'formidable' with 'a large stony jaw and furious black eyebrows'. • He is proud of his samurai ancestors. • He beat his son when he was a boy for talking too much. • He looks at Kikuko 'coldly'. • He wishes he had been a pilot during the war as there is 'always the final weapon'.
The father seems detached from his children.	• He alludes to what has happened in the past but never goes into detail. • He says he is prepared to forgive his son and blames whatever happened on others: 'You were swayed by certain – influences.' • He questions his daughter about Osaka and her university and she is very formal with him. • Kikuko will not smoke in front of him. • Kikuko says: 'You can never tell with Father.' • He says: 'Perhaps I should have been a more attentive father.' • He orders Kikuko to help him. • He waits for Kikuko to make the tea.
The father admired Mr Watanabe.	• He calls him 'A man of principle and honour'. • He says: 'I respected him very much'. • However, he says that the suicide was a mistake.
The father despises the modern world.	• He says that the world of business is very different from how it was in the past. • He does not wish to deal with foreigners. • He does not want to do things the way foreigners do them. • He does not understand why things have changed.

2 How would you describe the father? Arrange the following words in a diamond shape (1-2-3-2-1) with the most appropriate at the top and the least at the bottom.

sad	xenophobic	ethical
proud	honourable	traditional
lonely	domineering	cold

What evidence can you find in the text to support your choices?

Where does the story happen?

1 Ishiguro makes the **setting** interesting and convincing for readers who have never been to Japan.

a What information does he include about the house and garden?

b What information does he include about the father's special room?

c What do you think this special room tells the reader about the father?

Themes and ideas

You should remember that there is a difference between themes and ideas.

- **Themes** are the subjects that the short stories in *Telling Tales* are based on.
- **Ideas** are ways of understanding aspects of the themes.

The first section of 'A Family Supper', up until the arrival of Kikuko, introduces many of the themes and ideas of the story, for example honour, blame and guilt, death and the differences between parents and children.

The father clearly feels that honour is important and he tries to live his life by a code of honour – doing what he considers to be right in what he considers to be the right way.

1 Write brief answers to the following questions:

a What evidence can you find that the father is always polite?

b Why do you think he would be particularly proud of having samurai blood?

c What do you think the word '**pure**' implies about the samurai blood?

d What do you learn about the father's business and Mr Watanabe?

e What impression do you get of the father's opinion of Mr Watanabe's actions?

f What does it imply about the father that he did not follow Mr Watanabe's example?

The tea-room looked out over the garden. From where I sat I could make out the ancient well which as a child I had believed haunted.

It was an old woman. She was just standing there, watching me.

PUTTING DETAILS TO USE

Now that you have looked at the story more closely, you can use the details you have discovered to build the important skills you will need to explore the key areas of character, setting and ideas.

Exploring the characters, setting, ideas and feelings

1 What evidence can you find from the text to support the following interpretations of Kikuko's personality? Copy and complete the following table:

Kikuko	
Interpretation	**Evidence**
She is frightened of her father and does what he says.	
She is really pleased to see her brother after two years.	'Seeing me again seemed to make her excessively excited'
She is daring when away from home.	
She wants to be independent and make her own choices.	
She is friendly.	
She enjoys showing off.	
She is thoughtful.	
She finds it hard to accept her mother's death.	
She sometimes resents being ordered about by her father.	

2 A student was asked to write about the character of Kikuko. This is what they wrote:

Kikuko seems to be a little giddy because she giggles and grins a great deal but sometimes she appears to be very thoughtful, as when she is talking about her mother or when her father orders her about the kitchen. She is a bit of a rebel when she is away from home because she smokes, has a boyfriend and hitchhikes, but she is also careful to kick some pine needles over the end of her cigarette and she is not sure she wants to spend more time with her boyfriend. Sometimes she wants advice, for example when she asks her brother if she should go to California, and at other times she is very sure of her opinions, as when she describes the actions of Mr Watanabe in a single word – 'Sick'.

Using this interpretation of Kikuko as an example, write four sentences in response to each of the following tasks:

a   Describe, with supporting details, what the father is like.
b   Describe, with supporting details, the house and garden.
c   Describe some of the strong feelings and attitudes shown by the characters.

The narrator's standpoint

Both 'A Family Supper' and 'My Polish Teacher's Tie' are written as **first-person narratives**. The readers experience the narrative through the narrator's observations. However, the two stories are different. Carla Carter tells the reader of her own feelings, not just about other characters but also about herself.

This is not the case in 'A Family Supper'. In this story, the narrator merely observes: he does not make any judgements and he very rarely says what his own feelings are. This can make it difficult for the reader, who has to fill in the gaps where information about a character's feelings and judgements would normally be expected.

> ### ✔ Learning checkpoint
>
> Identify four pieces of evidence from the text that helped you to form an opinion of:
>
> - a character
> - the setting
> - a feeling or attitude.
>
> Write a sentence to explain how each piece of evidence supports your interpretation.

A panel would slide open and another room would appear. But the rooms were all startlingly empty.

How the characters are presented

Like John McGahern in 'Korea', Ishiguro does not present characters in a straightforward way. He rarely uses physical description and he often uses short sentences to tell the reader what they may be thinking or feeling.

Consider the way he creates the character of the mother, who is very influential in the story even though she is dead.

The reader first learns that the mother died through eating a fish and being poisoned. Ishiguro emphasises that eating the fish is very dangerous, that the victim '**rolls about in agony for a few hours**' and that the resulting death is '**hideously painful**'.

The reader has to wonder why the mother ate the fugu. The reason given (that she did not want to offend an old schoolfriend) seems a little odd, especially as she had always refused to eat it in the past. Ishiguro further confuses the reader by using the word '**Apparently**'. This may imply that this is something the narrator has been told but which may not necessarily be the case.

Ishiguro also indicates the breakdown in the family's relationships by stating that the narrator did not learn about the details of his mother's death for two years. It seems a considerable understatement when the narrator says that, '**My relationship with my parents had become somewhat strained**'.

Given the circumstances, it is also ironic that the father's first words in the story are, '**Did you eat on the plane?**' Soon after this he says, '**You must be hungry**', a statement he repeats twice more later in the story.

> **Watch an expert discuss key themes and ideas in the story on Cambridge Elevate.**

1 Working in a pair, read these quotations and then write notes in answer to the questions that follow:

'Your mother too was always ready to welcome you back – upset as she was by your behaviour.'

'Mother never really blamed you, you know … She always used to say to me how it was their fault, hers and Father's, for not bringing you up correctly.'

'… She had many worries. And some disappointments.'

a How does Ishiguro suggest that the mother's death might have been suicide?

b What do you learn about the relationship between the father and the mother?

c What evidence can you find from the story to support your opinions?

2 In an interview Ishiguro said:

The power relationships in Japanese family are actually very different from those that I have observed in Western families. It doesn't quite operate in the same way. The person who is directly in charge of the child is the mother. Very much so, more than in a Western family. Of course the father takes an interest, but educating the kids, bringing up the kids, is not in his realm.

To what extent do you think that Ishiguro has shown in the story that this is true of:

a the mother   **c** Mr Watanabe?
b the father

How the characters relate to each other

'She's a good girl.' The father says this about Kikuko on two separate occasions. Kikiko herself says about her mother, **'She used to tell me how much more careful they'd been with me, and that's why I was so good**.'

1 Working in a small group, hot-seat the character of Kikuko. Ask her about her life and her ideas about what she might do in the future.

Exploring themes and ideas

There are several references in the story to behaving in a morally correct and honourable way.

1 Working in a group, devise a series of questions for the following characters, which explore why they behaved in the ways they did:

a the father   **c** Kikuko
b the narrator   **d** Mr Watanabe.

2 Swap your questions with another group and then hot-seat the four characters to test how far they feel their actions were correct and honourable.

'She's a good girl,' my father said quietly.

75

'You must be hungry,' he said. One side of his face had fallen into shadow.

3 'I am – in retirement. I'm too old to involve myself in new ventures now.' How does the father respond to new ways of thinking and behaving? Make notes about:

- his wartime experience
- his business
- his reaction to the loss of his wife
- his reaction to the loss of his son
- his feelings about cooking
- his feelings about growing old.

4 'Perhaps I should have been a more attentive father.' What does this line imply about the father's thoughts?

5 The following examples of students' work show how you can develop your **understanding** into **interpretation** to **explore** other possible meanings. What differences do you notice in the three answers, in response to the following question?

How does the father relate to his children?

He says that Kikuko is a good girl and he asks her to help him in the kitchen. He is anxious to make his son welcome, takes him on a tour of the house and offers him food. ← *Shows understanding*

He thinks that Kikuko is a good girl who can be relied upon to help him with the cooking and to make tea when he tells her to even though she seems to resent this. He says that he has forgiven his son and he hopes that he will return to the family home. ← *Shows interpretation*

He believes that Kikuko is a good girl. This shows how little he understands his daughter. In reality she smokes, hitchhikes, has a boyfriend, is thinking of going to America and resents being ordered about like a servant. He appears to have forgiven his son for an action Ishiguro never reveals, saying 'You were swayed by certain – influences', although he does talk about how much the boy's mother was hurt by his leaving home. ← *Shows exploration*

Analysing language, form and structure

As with other stories in *Telling Tales*, there are important moments in 'A Family Supper' when nothing is actually said, but the silence can carry a variety of possible meanings.

1 Look at the following extract:

'I'm sorry to hear about the firm,' I said when neither of us had spoken for some time.

Here is a list of possible implications of this sentence. Rank them in order of probability and explain your choices:

a   The narrator is trying to break the silence by talking about something important.

b   The narrator is really sorry the firm has closed.

c   The father and the narrator have little to say to each other, even after a two-year absence.

d   The narrator is trying to make the father feel better about his failure.

e   The silence shows that the relationship remains damaged, even after a two-year absence.

2 What other moments of silence can you find in the story? Choose two examples and suggest what the characters might be thinking but not saying at that moment.

3 Re-read the section of the story where the narrator and Kikuko discuss the ghost in the garden. Then answer these questions:

a   How does Ishiguro show Kikuko's reactions to the ghost in the garden?

b   What else do the narrator and Kikuko discuss in this section of the story?

c   How do their memories of the ghost put these other things into perspective?

d   How does the ghost in the white kimono link to the mother?

e   Why do you think Ishiguro includes the ghost in the story?

Exploring a key moment in the story

The meal at the end of 'A Family Supper' begins with little conversation, darkness and formal politeness. It is clearly not a happy occasion in which a member of the family is welcomed home. Then the narrator notices a photograph at the back of the room.

The meal then continues with a surprise: the large pot that has been left unopened at the centre of the table contains fish. When questioned, the father says that it is '**Just fish.**'

1 Working in a group of six, look at the section beginning 'Who is that? In that photograph there?' up to "You must be hungry,' he said.'

Act out this scene with two people playing each character. One person should say the lines and act out the movements as they appear in the story; the other should say what the character is **really thinking** when they speak and when they move.

2 What does this part of the story imply about the relationships within the family?

3 Working in pairs, choose which you think is the most likely reason for the fact that fish is served at the meal. Justify your choice.

The serving of fish at the evening meal:

a   is a reminder of the mother's death and has been cooked by the father to make his children feel guilty they have let her down

b   shows that fish is a very popular meal in Japan

c   is a memorial to his wife – a statement that he misses her and expects his children to miss her too

d   attempts to shock the narrator into a realisation that he has effectively killed his mother by neglect

e   aims to give the reader a shock because it means that he might be serving fugu to do what Mr Watanabe did – kill himself and his family.

Learning checkpoint

In the character of the narrator, Ishiguro has created a young man who is an outsider. He has experienced life, and a relationship, in a very different country and has returned home for a reason that is never given.

1 Write brief notes on each of the following points, including relevant quotations from the story, to explore how Ishiguro presents:

- the narrator's relationship with his father
- what the narrator thinks of his sister
- what the narrator feels about his mother's death
- how the narrator feels about himself.

2 Use your notes to write a response of about 300 words to the following question: **What do you think the narrator feels about the consequences of his actions in the past?**

What are the author's intentions?

Look back at the notes you made about Japanese culture in the 'Getting started' section at the beginning of this unit. Kazuo Ishiguro has admitted that, in writing this story, he was setting out to challenge Western stereotypes about Japanese values. In one interview he said:

A while ago, I published a short story entitled 'A Family Supper'. The story was basically just a big trick, playing on Western readers' expectations about Japanese people who kill themselves.

In another interview, he made his intentions and methods clearer:

What the British make of it is a bit bizarre. They seem to think that Japanese people are dying to kill themselves … They like kamikaze and hara-kiri. I suppose in that story I was consciously playing on the expectations of a Western reader. You can trip the reader up by giving out a few omens. Once I set the expectation about the fugu fish up I found I could use that tension and that sense of darkness for my own purposes.

1 How do you think Ishiguro has played upon the Western reader's expectations of 'Japanese values' in this story? With a partner, discuss your own preconceptions of the following ideas and how Ishiguro has used them in his story:

- **a** the place of children in Japanese families
- **b** personal honour
- **c** family honour
- **d** honourable suicide.

2 When Ishiguro speaks about using stereotypes and expectations 'for my own purposes', what do you think these purposes might be?

GETTING IT INTO WRITING

As you have worked through this unit you have been building on your basic understanding of the story by analysing and interpreting the text. The next step is to develop your ideas and practise putting these together into a written response.

1 Use your ideas and notes from this unit to write a response to the following question:

> How do writers present death in 'A Family Supper' and in one other story from *Telling Tales*?
>
> Write about:
>
> - some of the ideas about death that are presented in the two stories
> - how the writers present these ideas by the ways they write.

 Complete this assignment on Cambridge Elevate.

Structuring your response

Remember the 'What' and the 'How':

- **What** are the ideas about death in these two stories? Of course the deaths the writers describe will be different in both stories, although bear in mind that they may have some things in common. For example they may be planned and considered suicides or sudden and completely unexpected accidents. They may have unexpected consequences.
- **How** do the writers convey these ideas in the language and structures they use in their stories? The writers' use of language and language devices may be very different, although you should also look for ways in which the stories are similar.

Choosing another story

You will first need to decide which of the other stories in *Telling Tales* you are going to write about.

You might consider writing about 'Chemistry'. There are several reasons why this might be a good choice. For example you could write about the deaths within the family unit in both stories or the possible ways in which two of the deaths might have been suicides or the ways in which the writers use ghosts. ('Korea' might also be a good choice because of the unexpected consequences of Luke Moran's death or the ways in which deaths in the past affect the characters in the present).

When you make your choice you might consider:

- the nature of the deaths themselves
- narrative voice
- uses of language and structure
- the attitudes of the writers.

For the **first** part of your response, you will need to bring together the notes you made earlier about the narrator and his father in 'A Family Supper'. These will help you to get started. Then look back at the notes you made for 'Chemistry'. In both cases you need to focus on the deaths that occur in the stories.

For the **second** part, you will need to write about the ways in which Ishiguro and Swift have used language and structure in their stories. For example you could write about:

- how the deaths are presented: Ishiguro presents the deaths of the Watanabe family through the father and the death of the narrator's mother through the narrator; Swift describes the three deaths in the story through the narrative voice of the young boy now grown up.
- how both writers explore the idea of suicide: for Mr Watanabe this was a way of following the code of the samurai. Perhaps it was the same for the narrator's mother or perhaps she chose not to continue living with her husband. For the grandfather in 'Chemistry', it is a way of escaping a life he no longer wishes to live.
- the ways in which both writers show the consequences of the deaths.

My father was ... particularly proud of the pure samurai blood that ran in the family.

Improving your response

1 Here are some extracts from students' responses to the question about death. Work with a partner to decide which extracts have gone beyond simple comments about the story to a convincing exploration of language or ideas.

2 Of the extracts below, only Student F's extract discusses more than one story. Choose one of the other responses and expand it to explore ideas about death in either 'Chemistry' or 'Korea'.

Student A

In 'A Family Supper' Mr Watanabe killed himself, his wife and his two little children after his business went broke. The narrator's mother has also died because she ate a poisonous fish.

Student B

In 'A Family Supper' the narrator, as a young boy, saw a ghost of an old woman in his garden. 'She was wearing a white kimono' and 'Some of her hair had come undone.' However, the reader is never really sure whether the narrator really did see the ghost. Kikuko says that he is just trying to frighten her all over again. Ishiguro suggests that it might have been in some way associated with their mother, even though she was alive when the narrator saw the ghost.

Student C

When Ishiguro's father figure tells his son, 'It's my belief that your mother's death was no accident' he directly raises the possibility that it was a deliberate act. The father continues to say that 'She had many worries. And some disappointments'. The short, fractured sentences create an effect of careful thought. Ishiguro is implying that the father blames the son for the death because the son is insensitive to the unnamed things he had done in the past, which caused his departure to America and his mother's grief. Ishiguro juxtaposes the thought that parents must always lose their

children 'to things they don't understand' with the observation that 'These little gunboats here could have been better glued'. The glue that should keep the boat (and by extension the family) together as a complete unit is clumsy and does not work properly.

Student D

The narrator in 'A Family Supper' had been away for two years and had not even been told the way in which his mother had died. This is very surprising, as you would think his father or his sister would have told him and that he would have gone back home for the funeral.

Student E

In 'A Family Supper' there is a difference of opinion about the deaths of the Watanabe family. The father in the story describes Mr Watanabe as 'A man of principle and honour'. Kikuko does not agree. She speaks of 'Those two beautiful little girls' and describes the whole thing as being 'sick'.

Student F

Both writers use setting in order to isolate a main, elderly, character. In both cases the writers place their characters in a small, self-contained space where they are able to find some sort of solace and self-expression away from the emotional restrictions they face in their homes. Both men, of course, are grieving for their wives. Ishiguro places the father in a house in which the rooms are 'startlingly empty' ('startlingly' indicating much more than surprise) and the walls are 'stark'. This appears to be a physical manifestation of the father's emotional bleakness following the death of his wife but Ishiguro then places the father in a very different setting: a room 'packed full of books and papers' indicating an interest in the world around him. The room has flowers and pictures. This is a pleasant, cared-for sanctuary, which suggests that the man's life, though contained, has continued and that he may have come to terms with the deaths around him.

3 Having thought about these extracts, go back to your own response. What could you do to improve it?

GETTING FURTHER

1 Choose six of the most important moments in the story and illustrate them in the style of a cartoon strip. Give each illustration a short caption.

You might like to use these manga (Japanese comic) images as inspiration.

2 Imagine that the narrator stays at home with the father and that Kikuko leaves for America. On her return two years later she and her brother meet up. Script or improvise their conversation, in which they explain what has happened to them over the past two years and what has become of their father.

3 In 'A Family Supper', Ishiguro plays upon Western stereotypes of Japanese behaviour. What stereotypes do you think people from other countries would have about the British?

6

Invisible Mass of the Back Row

Claudette Williams

Your progress in this unit:

- explore how Claudette Williams presents the thoughts and feelings of the characters
- understand how she presents themes and ideas
- explore the importance of context in a text
- explore and analyse how Williams' use of language and structure affects the reader
- develop your own interpretation of characters, relationships and events.

GETTING STARTED - THE STORY AND YOU

1 Many teachers now use seating plans in their classrooms. These are designed to help learning and are often changed.

a   If there was no seating plan, where would be your perfect place to sit in a normal classroom? Would you prefer the back or front (Did you know that very few questions are asked of pupils at the front of the room because nobody behind them can hear their answers?), by a window/ radiator or near to/far away from the door?

b   Do you prefer tables to be:

- in long lines all joined together facing the front
- in long lines but with spaces between individual tables
- in squares with some pupils on all sides of the table?

2 Which of the following statements do you think best describes people who sit on the back row?

a   They are highly motivated and very enthusiastic and love answering questions.
b   They want to talk about football.
c   They want to manicure their nails.
d   They want to chat to each other and text their friends.
e   They are waiting with tremendous patience for the teacher to say something interesting.

3 Test yourself. Which of these statements about Christopher Columbus are true?

a   On 12 October 1492 he landed on a Caribbean island.
b   On his first voyage he took men, women and children back to Spain to show them off. Within six months all were dead.
c   He planted sugar canes.
d   Almost all the people of the islands he discovered died as a result of the diseases he and his men brought with them.
e   Using guns and mastiffs trained to tear people apart, his men tortured, raped, burned and slaughtered the inhabitants in search of gold.
f   His discovery led to the establishment of the slave trade.
g   He died without having any idea of which part of the world he had discovered.

STORY ESSENTIALS

Who

Hortense, a young Jamaican girl
Aunt Salna
Miss Henderson, a teacher
The Education Inspector
Teacher Edwards
The lunch sellers
Lorna Phillips, a pupil in Jamaica
Cousy
Hortense's mother and father
Hortense's family and friends in Jamaica and England

When and where

The story is set in 1965 in Heartease, near Easington, Jamaica, and London, England.

Sequence of events

- The story begins in a school in Jamaica. A school Inspector asks Hortense, a girl on the back row, to speak about Christopher Columbus. She replies that she does not understand what Columbus was doing in the Caribbean. She is punished for her cheek.
- On the way to the hill where the pupils buy and eat their lunch, she chases Lorna Phillips, a pretty, rich girl with light skin.
- Hortense lives with her Aunt Salna. She arrives home to discover she and her brothers will be moving to England to live with their parents. Hortense is both scared and excited.
- When she arrives in England she is once again placed on the back row.
- Together with her friends, she begins to understand her heritage. The story ends with Hortense explaining what Columbus actually did – a victory for the back row.

Themes and ideas

- identity
- history
- stereotypes

- society
- immigration
- prejudice

- narrative voice
- power
- relationships

Contexts

Claudette Williams spent the first ten years of her life in Jamaica. For most of this time she lived with her Aunt Salna. In 1965 she moved to London to join her father, who had moved in 1957, and her mother, who had moved three years later.

My involvement in Black women's organizations consolidated further my class, race, and gender politics, and provided the interconnections for my individual situation with that of the oppression and exploitation of people generally thus strengthening the belief that politics is about struggle, which can never stop because it's also about survival.

'Gal, you come from foreign,' so aptly reflects my situation as a migrant to Britain.

GETTING CLOSER – FOCUS ON DETAILS

The following activities will help you develop your skills from understanding to interpreting. As you work through this unit, you will also progress from exploring to analysing the story. Keep your own notes as you work through the activities. You will use them to bring together your own written response to the story at the end of the unit.

What happens in the story?

Most of the first-person narrators in this Anthology – for example the boy in 'Chemistry' or Carla Carter in 'My Polish Teacher's Tie' – have been invented by the authors. This story is different, as many of the incidents described really happened to the writer, Claudette Williams. This makes the story both fictional and autobiographical.

1 Place these real events from the writer's life in the order in which they appear in the story.

  a   She learnt about Black History from books.
  b   She and her brother were reunited with her parents in 1965.
  c   She lived in Heartease, Jamaica.
  d   She was placed in band 5 in her new secondary school.
  e   Her father migrated to England in 1957 and her mother followed in 1960.
  f   When she came to England she was always cold.
  g   She lived in Jamaica with her Aunt Salna.
  h   When she was reunited with her mother she was not sure what to call her.

Understanding the characters

1 The story begins in a schoolroom, where an Inspector is visiting. Answer these questions.

  a   What is the role of the Inspector?
  b   Why are the pupils scared of him?
  c   How does Miss Henderson react to Hortense's answers?
  d   Why is Miss Henderson afraid?

2 What does the reader learn about Hortense in the first part of the story (up to lunchtime)?

3 Working with a partner, arrange the following words to describe Hortense in a diamond shape (1-2-3-2-1) with the most appropriate at the top and the least at the bottom.

daring	scared	clever
proud	powerful	observant
angry	rebellious	thoughtful

What evidence can you find to support your choices?

4 How does Hortense explain the fact that Lorna Phillips is on the front row?

5 What other reasons does Hortense have for not liking Lorna?

6 Why does Lorna Phillips say Hortense is on the back row?

7 In what ways is Teacher Edwards different from the other teachers?

Where does the story happen?

Williams creates a contrast between the controlled life of the classroom and the freedom and liveliness of the world beyond the classroom walls.

1 What impression do you get of the classroom and the school?

2 What details make the lunch women and Herby seem so pleasant when compared with Miss Henderson and the Inspector?

3 What details are provided about the house where Hortense lives?

4 What do you learn about her family?

 Listen to an extract from the story on Cambridge Elevate.

Themes and ideas

The first section of the story brings out the themes of education and power. The history lesson about Columbus being taught by Miss Henderson and tested by the Inspector does not tell the whole story of what happened. Columbus and his adventures are taught simply as a list of dates and the names of ships – at least that is what Miss Henderson and the Inspector expect the pupils to know. They are not teaching the pupils about what Columbus really did to the lands and people he 'discovered'.

In an autobiographical essay, Claudette Williams explains the difference between skin colour in 1960s Jamaica:

My school experience reinforced colourism. It taught me that it was the fair skinned children who received praise and the teacher's attention, and the Black children who were relegated to the back of the classroom.

In the story, we are told what Hortense's uncle feels about education:

My uncle say all a dem collude to humiliate, not just me, but all a we, all de people who look like me. All de poor black people dem. Meck him no pick pan de red pickney dem, a meck him t'ink say is we alone no know nothing.

1. The Inspector is a representative of the government. He is there to make sure government rules are being obeyed.

   a How do the teachers in the school keep order?
   b Why do you think they teach one particular version of the history of their island?
   c Why do you think the government wants Jamaicans to learn this version of history?

2. What attitude does Hortense's uncle have towards education and the government? Do you have sympathy for his attitude? Explain your reasons.

Our senses are assaulted by saltfish fritters, fried dumplings, red herring, cornmeal pudding, sweet potato pudding, oranges, plums, mangoes or sugar-cane, snowball and sky-juice.

PUTTING DETAILS TO USE

Now that you have looked at the story more closely, you can use the details you have discovered to build the important skills you will need to explore the key areas of character, **setting** and ideas.

Exploring the characters, setting, ideas and feelings

1 In this story Williams is writing about herself when she was a young girl. She is doing this through a character she calls Hortense. What evidence can you find to support the following interpretations of Hortense's personality in the first part of the story (until she leaves for England)?

  a   She is daring.
  b   She does not have much respect for education.
  c   She is scared of her aunt.
  d   She hates anything that she thinks is unfair.
  e   She is something of a bully.
  f   She wants to go to England.
  g   She is both excited and scared about leaving Jamaica.

2 Re-read the section that describes the death of Cousy (starting 'Cousy had not moved, as she always did …').

Working in a small group, decide what this memory adds to the reader's understanding of Hortense.

3 A student was asked to write about the character of Miss Henderson. This is what they wrote:

Miss Henderson is shown to be a bad teacher, who can only control her pupils by fear when she uses her ruler to punish them. She is also described as being unattractive, having a 'sharp pointed nose' and 'mean eyes' giving her a witch-like appearance. However, she is also shown to be frightened of losing her job ('She is as much afraid of the Inspector as I am') if her pupils do not give the expected answers.

Using this interpretation of Miss Henderson as an example, write four sentences in response to each of the following tasks.

  a   Describe, with supporting details, what Hortense is like.
  b   Describe, with supporting details, the hillside at lunchtime and what it is like.
  c   Describe some of the strong feelings and attitudes shown by Hortense, her aunt and her uncle.

Who will look after Cousy's grave? Who will make sure that the weeds do not choke her roses?

✔ Learning checkpoint

Identify four pieces of evidence from the text that helped you to form an opinion of one of the following:

- a character
- the setting
- a feeling or attitude.

Write a sentence to explain how each piece of evidence supports your interpretation.

Watch an expert discuss key themes and ideas in the story on Cambridge Elevate.

The narrator's standpoint

'Invisible Mass of the Back Row' is written as a **first-person narrative** from the point of view of a young Hortense. The reader follows her experiences through her observations, attitudes, feelings and judgements. As with the character of Carla in 'My Polish Teacher's Tie', we respond well to Hortense's honesty and sympathise with the position she finds herself in. We trust that she is a reliable narrator and we believe what she says.

What the characters say and do

Claudette Williams creates an impression of the main character in the opening paragraphs, where Hortense is being tested by the school Inspector.

One student **annotated** the third paragraph of the story like this:

Annotation	Text
Simple sentence for emphasis – shows fear	Heat makes the scene more unpleasant; more pressure on Hortense
Metal – room is built like an oven. Poor buildings for pupils? Not valued?	Even more pressure
Sense of community – they are all scared	Shows Inspector is powerful and pupils powerless
Not seen as worthy of attention	Like an object – rubbish
These pupils don't count – not seen and not individuals; back row has some sort of group identity	Like a parcel
	Will soon be over – sense of doom

> My heart pounds. The heat of the morning sun, soaking through the galvanised roof, is magnified inside the schoolroom. The stench of fear is in everyone's nostrils. Something tells me that my days of being hidden, disposed of, dispatched to the invisibility of the back row, are numbered.

1 Annotate a copy of the two paragraphs that describe Hortense dressing on her last morning in Jamaica (from 'Like a stranger' to 'this familiar, tiny, two-roomed house') to show how Williams creates a feeling of sympathy for Hortense.

How the characters are presented

Claudette Williams presents all the other characters in the story through the eyes of Hortense: the reader sees what she sees and thinks what she thinks.

1 Look at the description of her new English school experience in the paragraph starting 'My strategic location in one five has a familiar feel about it'. Then, with a partner, answer the following questions:

a   What are the main activities of the girls?

b   Why do you think they have their own section of the common-room?

c   What do the smells of their section of the common-room tell you about the girls (note: Woolworth's was a popular High Street chain store that sold goods cheaply)?

d   How does this make the reader feel about Hortense and her friends?

e   Are there any other details that Williams uses to make the reader sympathetic or unsympathetic to the girls?

Exploring themes and ideas

As in 'My Polish Teacher's Tie', there are several references to language in this story. The way in which someone uses language is part of their identity, as well as part of their culture. The use and purpose of language will be different, depending on the **context**. For example young people talk to each other in ways that would not be appropriate if talking to someone older, like a teacher; and language used in social media is very different from language used for writing essays about literature.

Hortense uses a Jamaican **patois** (a form of non-standard language). At times this makes what she says hard for some readers to understand. It also shows her pride in her cultural identity.

When she was in school, Claudette Williams enjoyed reading and discovered a range of novels about slaves. She said:

Racist, sexist, and totally Eurocentric as they were, they unfolded for me the brutality and painful historical exploitation of slavery. These books made me angry, disgusted, and outraged. How could such barbaric acts be romanticized?

The discovery of new heroes, rebels and guerrilla fighters in the books the pupils read is significant in the story.

1 What is the effect on the reader of the following statements?

Words fail to come out.

Words gush out of my mouth.

The silence of parting quiets the most active tongue.

I fell back on old responses, familiar language.

No one told me I would need a new language in dis England.

Here I was without a language to reply to her calls.

I said all of this slowly, so that I would say it well.

Voices are raised, claiming, proclaiming, learning the new language in dis here England.

2 Working in a small group, rank the following statements (in order of importance) about Hortense's use of language. Explain the reasons for your ranking order.

a She finds it difficult to talk to adults, even her own mother.
b She finds it very hard to move from Jamaica to England because people use language in different ways.
c She speaks very quickly when she gets excited.
d She finds it difficult to be quiet.
e She is aware that some people look down on her language because it is not standard English.

3 The following examples of students' work show how you can develop your **understanding** into **interpretation** to **explore** other possible meanings. What differences do you notice in the three answers, in response to the following question?

How does language contribute to Hortense's sense of her own identity?

She speaks one type of language in Heartease and finds it difficult to adapt to a different kind of language in Britain.

Shows understanding

The ways in which she has difficulty in using language are shown when she calls her own mother 'Salna'. Her mother deals with the situation very tactfully, giving Hortense three choices of what to call her parents. However, the mistake shows that Hortense is having difficulty in establishing a new relationship with the parents she has not known for many years. She says she 'fell back on old responses, familiar language' because she does not feel she can acquire the new language that she thinks she now needs.

Shows interpretation

Throughout the story Williams uses language as a way of creating an identity for Hortense. She begins in silence, being unable to answer the Inspector's questions and then, when angry, words 'gush' from her mouth. At the end of the story she speaks very slowly 'so that I say it well' because the explanation of her cultural heritage is important to her and her friends on the back row. It is now the teacher who is silent as the class 'whoops' down the corridor, having affirmed the value of its cultural identity.

Shows exploration

Key terms

patois: the dialect of people from a particular area or region.
standard English: the variety of English used in public communication.

'What was Columbus doing here anyway?' The trapped words inside my head tumble out. The rebel inside me is alive.

We discover heroes, rebels, guerrilla fighters. They help us assert our right to be.

Sojourner Truth

4 Working in a small group, research the key points about the life of one of the following historical figures:

- Toussaint L'Ouverture (the name means 'someone who finds an opening') from Haiti
- Sojourner Truth, an American slave who fought for the abolition of slavery
- Cudjoe and his sister Nanny of the Maroons from Jamaica
- Paul Bogle, a Jamaican minister.

a Prepare a short presentation on your chosen historical figure.

b In what ways do these figures become important to Hortense, Fay Green and their friends?

c Why do you think Claudette Williams includes these people in her story?

Analysing language, form and structure

To mark Hortense's journey from one place to another, Williams uses a short poem as a means of dividing the story.

1 Working with a partner, annotate a copy of the poem to illustrate how Williams uses language to create a sense of contrast between the two settings.

Paraffin heaters
smell
always just coming
into cold dark places
afraid and
excited at the same
time
cold
smell
wanting to be elsewhere
in fact Jamaica

2 With a partner, rank the following statements that pupils have written about the poem. Rank them according to how well they explore the use of language to create an effect on the reader. Justify your decisions.

A *The poem is written by Hortense and is very direct, as the reader would expect. She contrasts the heat of Jamaica with the coldness of England by repeating the word 'cold'.*

B *The paraffin heater becomes a symbol of her feelings about life in her new home: it is cold and inhospitable and she finds it frightening. Later in the story she huddles by the paraffin heater when she speaks to her mother. These heaters were large and smelly and gave off an unpleasant heat.*

C In the poem Hortense says that she wants to go back to Jamaica because it is not a cold dark place.

D Williams uses the poem to show the Hortense's conflicting feelings: she is 'afraid and excited at the same time' – aware of what she has left behind but now looking to the future. The poem is simple and uses no punctuation. The short lines make it look disjointed and fractured and so mirror what Hortense is feeling.

Exploring a key moment in the story

The moment when Hortense and her mother visit Devon Spencer School is an important point in the story. It is Hortense's first contact with the British educational system and reveals some of its flaws.

1 Re-read the paragraph (from 'Mum came with me' down to 'the remedial stream'). Make notes on the following questions:

a How does Hortense's mother try to help her daughter?
b Do you think the Headmistress helps Hortense? If so, how?
c How does Williams use **irony** in this description?
d How does she make use of **slang**?
e Do you think this is a good way of introducing someone to a new school? Why, or why not?

Symbolism

In 'My Polish Teacher's Tie', Stefan's tie was a symbol of his own identity as a free spirit and also showed something about Mrs Kenward's snobbish attitudes to him. In 'Invisible Mass of the Back Row', clothing is also important.

1 In a small group, discuss these quotations about clothing and make notes to help you answer the questions that follow them.

He is handsomely dressed in his Dashiki suit.

Wash-rags, carried on shoulders like a uniform, mop brows

Like a stranger, I greet my new clothes, gingerly feeling, inhaling the new cloth smells. I try to work out which piece to put on first without disturbing my newly crafted hairstyle.

My brothers and I are ceremoniously handed over to a pretty, chocolate-coloured woman dressed in a blue uniform.

I sit huddled in strange clothes, close to the paraffin heater.

a How may clothing be related to location?
b How may clothing reveal social status?
c How may clothing be something that reveals attitudes?

🔑 Key terms

slang: informal language.

handsomely dressed in his Dashiki suit

Learning checkpoint

Claudette Williams often describes people's features and clothes to suggest what type of person they are.

1 Write two or three sentences about each of the following characters. Using relevant quotations, explain how Williams uses physical description to create character.

   a Miss Henderson

   b Miss Mavis

   c Cousy

   d Hortense's mother

   e the English teacher.

2 The author's choice for the title of a story is significant, and can carry a lot of meaning.

   a Think about the title of this story. What are the **connotations** of the following words/phrases:

   - Invisible
   - Mass
   - Back Row?

   b Think of an alternative title for the story that includes these connotations.

GETTING IT INTO WRITING

As you have worked through this unit, you have been building on your basic understanding of the story by analysing and interpreting the text. The next step is to develop your ideas and practise putting these together into a written response.

1 Use your ideas and notes from this unit to write a response to the following question:

How do writers present characters developing their sense of their own identities in 'Invisible Mass of the Back Row' and in one other story from *Telling Tales*?

Write about:

- some of the ideas about discovering identities that are presented in the two stories
- how the writers present these ideas by the ways they write.

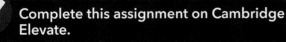

Complete this assignment on Cambridge Elevate.

Structuring your response

Remember the 'What' and the 'How':

- The 'What' is the 'ideas' about characters 'developing their sense of their own identities'.
- The 'How' is the writer's way of conveying those things through language and language devices.

Choosing another story

You should first decide which of the other stories in *Telling Tales* you are going to write about. You have already explored the character of Carla in 'My Polish Teacher's Tie'. This would be a good choice, as Carla rediscovers her Polish roots and joins Stefan in the song at the end of the story to celebrate her newly discovered identity.

For the **first** part of your response, you will need to bring together notes you made earlier about Hortense and Carla. These will help you to get started. Remember that you are exploring how their sense of themselves changes – they become a new person during the course of the stories. Alternatively, you could explore how both Carla and Hortense think they are 'invisible' to other people.

For the **second** part, you will need to write about the ways in which Dunmore and Williams have used language and structure in their stories.

You might want to consider:

- the importance of language in these two stories. It is through language that both characters find their identity. Both speak two languages: Carla speaks English and Polish; Hortense speaks Caribbean patois and standard English.
- the ways in which both writers suggest that schools and teachers are forces that prevent – rather than encourage – the characters to develop as individuals.
- the ways in which both writers use books as a means to help explore and establish identities. For Carla, the poems she reads from Steve and in the book that she bought are important in helping her to connect with the part of her that is Polish; for Hortense and her friends, books on Afro-Caribbean history help them establish their pride in their Black heritage.

> 🔑 **Key terms**
>
> **connotation:** an idea or a feeling linked to the main meaning of a word – what it implies or suggests in addition to its literal meaning.

Things mingle and whirl in my mind. Easington heat. Easington sweat. English cold. English ice. Frozen faces, frozen information, frozen places.

Improving your response

1 Here are some extracts from students' responses to the question about identities in 'Invisible Mass of the Back Row'. Work with a partner to decide which extracts have gone beyond simple comments about the story to a convincing exploration of language or ideas.

2 Choose two of these responses and expand them to explore identities in 'My Polish Teacher's Tie'.

Student A

Claudette Williams considers the idea of humiliation through educational racism. In Jamaica, the pupils in the back row walk down the hill to the lunch sellers in 'The gloom of humiliation, the pain of the assault on all of us'. Here Williams suggests that the pain is not because one person has been hit by a ruler ('One little ruler slap a nothing', as Hortense says) but that the educational system has conspired to humiliate 'not just me, but all a we' as her uncle says. The system has been created to keep poor Afro-Caribbeans in their place. In the end Hortense triumphs over these humiliations and the reader is left thinking that she will now have a better future, secure in an understanding of her identity and heritage.

Student B

Hortense is a very proud young girl. She sometimes says things that annoy her teachers but this does not stop her saying them. She has a hard life in Jamaica because living with her aunt is not easy.

Student C

Teachers in Jamaica and England seem to be a pretty dreadful bunch. In Jamaica, Miss Henderson rules by fear and is described in unpleasant terms with her 'wrinkled forehead', 'sharp pointed nose' and 'mean eyes'. Her appearance shows her character: she is indeed mean and is unable to teach anything that is not laid down by the government rules. As a consequence, her teaching of history is biased and untruthful.

Student D

Williams ends her story with Hortense's proud statement, 'Voices are raised, claiming, proclaiming, learning the new language in dis here England.' She is speaking on behalf of all her friends – the Afro-Caribbean girls on the back row who have come to symbolise all the migrants to England. Now the back row can feel a pride in their heritage. This is shown in the use of 'claiming, proclaiming', which shows firstly that they have understood and accepted their heritage and secondly that they take pride in it. The most interesting element of the sentence is William's use of 'dis here'. The use of a non-standard form implies that both standard and non-standard uses of language are of equal value and that England needs to accommodate them both.

Student E

Hortense lives with her aunt in Jamaica. Her mother and father have been living and working in England for some years. They send for her and she thinks that England is very cold. She is put into set five where she quickly makes new friends. She likes being on the back row.

Student F

Hortense knows that she will get into trouble with Miss Henderson and the Inspector when she asks 'What was Columbus doing here anyway?' but she cannot help herself. She feels that her brains are 'goading' her on, because she feels that she has to make some sort of comment on how Columbus caused nothing but death and destruction.

3 Having thought about these extracts, go back to your own response. What could you do to improve it?

GETTING FURTHER

1 Working in a small group, script or improvise a TV interview with Hortense, now an adult, which looks back over her childhood and her experience of coming to Britain to join her parents in London. Your questions should cover:

- what actually happened to her
- how she felt about her experiences at the time (for example how she felt joining parents she did not know and how she was treated by the educational system in both Jamaica and Britain)
- how she feels about her experiences now she is an adult.

2 Imagine that her English teacher has asked Hortense to write a message to her future self. In the message she should:

- explain what her life is like as a Jamaican living in London (going to school, sitting on the back row and teaching herself about her heritage)
- describe the sort of person she wants to become when she is older (her hopes, fears and aspirations for the future, not just for herself but for the country where she is living).

3 Share your messages with a partner. Then discuss what you think might have happened to Hortense.

Voices are raised, claiming, proclaiming, learning the new language in dis here England.

7

The Darkness Out There

Penelope Lively

Your progress in this unit:

- explore how Penelope Lively presents characters and their thoughts and feelings
- develop your own interpretation of characters, relationships and events
- understand how Lively presents themes and ideas
- explore and analyse how Lively's use of language and structure affects the reader
- develop your written response skills.

GETTING STARTED – THE STORY AND YOU

1 Which of the following would come closest to your reaction if you saw this notice in your school library?

Come and have fun giving a helping hand to the old folks.

Adopt a granny

a That sounds like a fun idea. I'll ask my best friend to come as well.

b Gross! There is as much chance of a dragon ridden by a pixie winning the Grand National as me giving a helping hand.

c It is terrible that society no longer looks after our ageing population but relies on untrained and unpaid child workers.

d That would look good on my CV and might help me get an internship when I finish university.

e What goes around comes around. We're all going to grow old. If I look after someone now, maybe someone will look after me when my time comes.

2 Write your own fairy tale:

- **Choose a time and a place.** This can be mystical or realistic, in the past or the future.
- **Choose three characters.** At least one should be 'good' and another 'evil'.
- **Decide on a theme.** This can be a moral or a message.
- **Write the plot outline in bullet points.** Remember you need a beginning (setting up the characters and place), a middle (a difficult or dangerous situation) and an end (a resolution of the problem, possibly a death).
- **Think of a good beginning.** For example 'In the middle of a dark forest there was a crooked little house.'
- **Think of a good ending.** For example 'You must always be careful what you wish for.'
- **Finally…** Tell your story to other people to see what they think of it.

STORY ESSENTIALS

Who

Major characters
Sandra, a teenage girl
Kerry, a teenage boy
Mrs Rutter, an elderly woman

Minor characters
Pat, organiser of the Good Neighbours' Club
Dot, Mrs Rutter's sister
A young German airman

When and where

The story takes place in the late 20th century in and around Mrs Rutter's home, Nether Cottage at Packer's End.

Sequence of events

- As part of her school's Good Neighbours' Club, Sandra is sent to visit Mrs Rutter at Nether Cottage in Packer's End.
- Sandra has heard rumours about the dark woods of Packer's End, including wild animals, rapists and German airmen.
- On the way, she thinks about her future life, envisioning a little white house and a family. Her thoughts are interrupted by Kerry Stevens, a boy she does not like.
- After Sandra and Kerry have done some household tasks for Mrs Rutter, she tells them about a German plane that crashed in the woods during the war. One of the airmen had survived but was badly injured. Mrs Rutter gives a number of reasons why she and her sister did not help him. He took two days to die.
- Kerry is both shocked and angry. He leaves. Sandra follows. Sandra begins to realise that the real darkness is not to be found in woods but in people.

Themes and ideas

- innocence
- fear
- stereotypes
- evil
- pretence
- maturity
- narrative voice
- relationships
- how the past affects the present

Contexts

Penelope Lively was born in Cairo, Egypt, in 1933 and moved to England when she was 12. She has won awards for her children's books, including *The Ghost of Thomas Kempe* and *A Stitch in Time*, and for her novels for adults, such as *Moon Tiger*. This short story was written in 1984.

Children are not like us … They inhabit not our world but a world we have lost and can never recover. We do not remember childhood – we imagine it. We search for it, in vain, through layers of obscuring dust, and recover some bedraggled shreds of what we think it was. And all the while the inhabitants of this world are among us, like aborigines, like Minoans, people from elsewhere safe in their own time-capsule.

GETTING CLOSER – FOCUS ON DETAILS

The following activities will help you develop your skills from understanding to interpreting. As you work through this unit, you will also progress from exploring to analysing the story. Keep your own notes as you work through the activities. You will use them to bring together your own written response to the story at the end of the unit.

 Listen to an extract from the story on Cambridge Elevate.

What happens in the story?

The structure of the story seems very simple:

- Sandra and Kerry go to Mrs Rutter's cottage and do some jobs for her.
- Mrs Rutter tells them a story about what happened in the war.
- Sandra and Kerry leave.

The story is a **third-person narrative**. The reader sees the events through Sandra's eyes and is sometimes allowed to share her thoughts, for example when she daydreams about going '**to places like on travel brochures**' and running '**into a blue sea**'.

However, there is more to the story than Sandra's experience of it. The reader is made to wonder what other characters might think about the visit to Nether Cottage and the revelation about what happened in the woods during the war.

1 Working with a partner, script or improvise a conversation in which Kerry Stevens tells old Bill at the garage about his visit to Mrs Rutter's cottage and what happened there.

2 Again working with a partner, script or improvise a conversation between Mrs Rutter and Pat in which they discuss the visit by Sandra and Kerry.

3 At first the story appears to be a modern fairy tale. For example Sandra is sent on a mission and she finds a companion along the way.

    a   Which other parts of the story are like a fairy tale?
    b   Which fairy tales do they remind you of?
    c   Which parts of the story are not like a fairy tale?

Understanding the characters

Many of the characters in 'The Darkness Out There' are described by their appearances and clothes, which sometimes reveal something about their characters. For example Mrs Carpenter at the King's Arms has '**platinum highlights and spike heel suede boots**'. Sandra observes that she is very different from Pat and seems to admire Mrs Carpenter's looks. The reader is led to think that one day Sandra too would like platinum highlights and spike heel boots to replace her sandals.

One day, this year, next year sometime, she would go to places like on travel brochures and run into a blue sea.

She would walk like this through the silken grass with the wind seething the corn

1 Look again at the second paragraph of the story. What physical description is given of Pat Hammond?

2 The description of Pat is seen through Sandra's eyes. Which of the following statements best sums up Sandra's view of Pat at this point in the story? Give reasons for your answer.

a She should take more care over her appearance.
b People who help others are shabbily dressed.
c Appearances can reveal character.
d Pat's appearance is unfortunate.
e Jerseys shouldn't be washed too many times.

3 What physical details can you find that describe Kerry Stevens? Complete a table like the following one with evidence from the story.

Kerry's physical attributes	How are they described?
Hair	
Eyes	
Chin	
Stomach	
Fingers	

4 At the end of the story the reader is told that Kerry:

had grown; he had got older and larger. His anger eclipsed his acne

What do you think has made this happen?

5 Working with a partner use the following mind map to write around 100 words on Sandra's appearance. Use quotations from the text to support what you write.

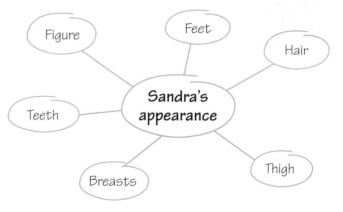

6 What kind of a person is Sandra? Arrange the following words in a diamond shape (1-2-3-2-1) with the most appropriate at the top and the least appropriate at the bottom.

self-centred	kind	naive
judgemental	nervous	shallow
narcissistic	idealistic	selfish

Find evidence to support your choices.

> She wouldn't go in there for a thousand pounds,
> not even in bright day like now, with nothing
> coming out of the dark slab of trees but birdsong

Where does the story happen?

Penelope Lively places Mrs Rutter in a small rundown cottage at the edge of a mysterious wood. She is well away from the rest of the world. It is almost as though she were in a fairy tale.

1 What details does Lively give you about the woods in Packer's End?

2 Does she make them seem welcoming, mysterious or threatening?

3 What do young children think might happen in the woods?

4 What do older children think might happen?

5 Why do you think it is important that Nether Cottage is on the edge of Packer's End?

6 What might the name 'Nether' imply about the cottage?

Themes and ideas

The first section of the story gives us the impression that Sandra takes people at face value. She believes that people are as they appear to be: Pat is dowdy and to be pitied; Mrs Carpenter is sexy and to be admired; Kerry is not up to much and to be avoided.

She believes that the wood is full of danger, and when she was young she believed in witches and wolves. These fears were replaced by a fear of rapists ('**Two enormous blokes, sort of gypsy types.**') These fears are based on rumour and hearsay ('**people at school said**') and the reader is made to think that they have no truth behind them – they are just figments of young peoples' over-active imaginations.

At the end of the story, Sandra has realised that there is no threat or darkness in the woods themselves. Rather, she realises it is people who can be evil. Little old ladies are as capable of committing evil as anyone else. It is the seemingly ordinary people who are 'The Darkness'.

1 Re-read the three paragraphs about Packer's End (starting 'When they were small').

   a Why do you think the young children were afraid of the witches, wolves and tigers?

   b Why did they go into the woods for a dare?

   c What did the young children feel afterwards?

   d What details of the attack and rape on the girl is the reader given?

   e What references to darkness can you find in these paragraphs?

   f What is the effect of these references to darkness on the reader?

PUTTING DETAILS TO USE

Now that you have looked at the story more closely, you can use the details you have discovered to build the important skills you will need to explore the key areas of character, **setting** and ideas.

Exploring the characters, setting, ideas and feelings

1 Re-read the paragraph starting 'She put her sandal back on'.

a What **six** different aspirations for the future does Sandra have?

b Where would you place Sandra on each of the scales shown below?

c In what ways do you share any of Sandra's aspirations?

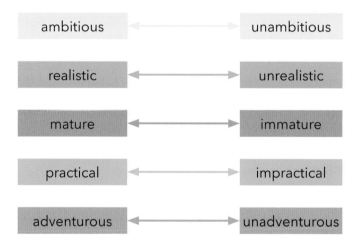

ambitious	unambitious
realistic	unrealistic
mature	immature
practical	impractical
adventurous	unadventurous

2 With a partner, make a table like the following one to explore Sandra's attitudes and feelings throughout the story. Which statements are true and which are false? What evidence can you find to support your decisions?

Character trait	True/False	Evidence
She is a very mature and helpful young woman who always puts others first.		
She is very arrogant and looks down on other people for no good reason.		
She is highly strung and imagines dangers where none exist.		
She is distressed by what she learns about the nature of evil.		
She is very vain and thinks that she is beautiful.		
She is highly immature and her future aspirations are just **clichés**.		
She is very pleased with herself – that's why she joined the Good Neighbours.		
She is easily shocked and just as easily impressed.		
She is becoming increasingly aware of her own sexuality.		
She grows up during the story and changes her attitudes.		

 Key terms

cliché: a very overused or unoriginal phrase.

3 A student was asked to write about Kerry. This is what they wrote:

> When he is introduced, Kerry jumps out and gives Sandra 'the fright of her life'. Unlike Sandra, he is physically unattractive and she assumes that 'Some people you only have to look at to know they're not up to much' – an assumption that she will later realise is wrong. It is Kerry who first reacts to Mrs Rutter's story and does so in a way that is quietly dignified and in Sandra's eyes demonstrates that he has grown in authority and that 'You could get people all wrong'. Just like Mrs Rutter, Kerry is not all that he seems.

Using this interpretation of Kerry as an example, write four sentences for the following tasks:

a   Describe, with supporting details, what Sandra is like.
b   Describe, with supporting details, Mrs Rutter's cottage.
c   Describe some of the feelings and attitudes shown by Sandra.

✔ **Learning checkpoint**

Identify four pieces of evidence from the text that helped you to form an opinion of:

- a character
- the setting of the story
- a feeling or attitude.

Write a sentence to explain how the evidence you chose supports your interpretation.

The narrator's standpoint

'The Darkness Out There' is a third-person narrative. The reader is told the story by an impersonal narrator but is also given access to Sandra's thoughts. She is a rather immature girl who is quick to make judgements and whose instincts can be wrong. This means that the reader cannot rely on her to be objective.

What the characters say and do

At first, Penelope Lively appears to present Kerry Stevens as a rather unpleasant-looking boy whom Sandra would prefer to avoid. He is dirty and enjoys giving her a fright. But, as we learn at the end of the story, everything is not as it seems.

Kerry's good qualities are gradually revealed through the course of the story. He is kind: he has volunteered for the Good Neighbours Club, although he just shrugs when Sandra mentions this, and he offers her a bit of his chocolate bar. Even though Mrs Rutter cannot be bothered to remember his name, he is rather more helpful than Sandra. He does the garden and fetches the kindling. He does not say very much, so his reaction to Mrs Rutter's story is shocking when it explodes.

1 Working with a partner, note down what you think Kerry is thinking when he says the things quoted in the table:

Quotation	Kerry's thoughts and feelings
'What was it? Messerschmitt?'	
'But either way …'	
'The other one?'	
'You what?'	
'I'm going,' 'Dunno about you, but I'm going.'	
'I'm not going near that old bitch again.'	
'Two bloody nights. Christ!'	

📹 **Watch an expert discuss key themes and ideas in the story on Cambridge Elevate.**

2 As with the other stories in the Anthology, for example 'Korea' and 'A Family Supper', silences are important.

What is Kerry thinking at these points in the story?

a The boy stared at her over the rim of the cup, blank-faced.
b The boy's spoon clattered to the floor; he did not move.

How the characters are presented

At first sight, it appears that Mrs Rutter really is the '**dear old thing**' Pat believes her to be. Lively describes her as being large: '**composed of circles, a cottage-loaf of a woman**'. One especially striking description is '**Mrs Rutter's smiles folded into one another**', which makes her seem to be a jolly, harmless little old lady. She also compliments Sandra on her prettiness.

However, Lively provides the reader with suggestions that Mrs Rutter is not what she may appear. She may say '**my eyesight's past it now, of course**' but her eyes are the key to her character.

1 Working with a partner, note down what Lively is suggesting about Mrs Rutter at these points in the story:

a A creamy smiling pool of a face in which her eyes snapped and darted.
b She glittered at them from the stove.
c Her eyes investigated, quick as mice.
d Above them, her eyes examined him.
e Mrs Rutter watched her come in, glinting from the cushions.
f Mrs Rutter licked her lips; she looked across at them, her eyes darting.

Her eyes investigated, quick as mice.

Exploring themes and ideas

The central theme of the story is 'The Darkness' – the idea that evil is not a matter of creatures and people lurking in the woods of fairy tales but rather of actions committed by ordinary people behaving in inhumane ways.

Mrs Rutter and her sister Dot left a young German airman to die when they might have been able to save him. Mrs Rutter gives a number of reasons for this:

- The weather was bad: '**rain teeming down and a raw November night**'.
- It was wartime and the Germans were the enemy: '**and a good job too, three of them that'll be**'.
- Dot was feeling poorly: '**running a bit of a temp, she had the 'flu or something coming on**'.
- Mrs Rutter's bike had a puncture.
- Mrs Rutter's husband had been killed: '**I thought, why should I do anything for you? Nobody did anything for my Bill, did they?**'

1 What do you think of these reasons for doing nothing to rescue the German airman?

2 Look again at the parts of the story where Mrs Rutter describes the young airman. How does Lively make the reader feel sympathy for him?

3 The following examples of students' work show how you can develop your **understanding** into **interpretation** to **explore** other possible meanings. What differences do you notice in the three answers, in response to the following question?

How right is Kerry when he calls Mrs Rutter 'that old bitch'?

He has listened to her story and thinks that what she and her sister did was evil.

> Shows understanding

He has listened to her story and thinks that she acted in an evil way by leaving the German airman to die slowly and in agony when she could have tried to save him. This, he thinks, was cruel and means that Mrs Rutter is evil, even though it happened many years ago.

> Shows interpretation

He has listened to her story and has been increasingly shocked by it, so shocked that his spoon clatters to the floor and he is unable to say anything. As Mrs Rutter reveals what happened that night and during the next day he remains silent but then stands up and simply announces that he is leaving. Only after he is out of the house does he explode with anger at what he has heard. And yet the reader may feel that perhaps Mrs Rutter was right when she said 'Tit for tat' and that she was exacting a sort of revenge for the death of her husband, 'a lovely man'.

> Shows exploration

Analysing language, form and structure

As you have seen in other stories from the Anthology, the ways in which places are described can be very important. For example in 'Chemistry' Graham Swift describes the loneliness and desolation of the pond and the warmth of the Grandfather's shed, and in 'A Family Supper' Ishiguro creates a contrast between the empty house and the room where his father keeps his papers and models. In 'The Darkness Out There', the journey to Nether Cottage, through the '**rank place**' with its saplings and brambles and dumped furniture, **foreshadows** the events that are to occur.

> **Key terms**
>
> **foreshadow:** to hint at what lies ahead, often in the sense of a warning.

A student has **annotated** the following paragraph to show how the setting contributes to the story as well as what Sandra wishes her future life will hold. This is in contrast to the garden of Nether Cottage.

Annotations (left):

- Hard sound, creates unpleasant image; manmade
- Contrast of reality of compost heap with S's vision of ideal rural life
- Repetition to emphasise distaste; same sound as 'wincing'. Hard – hurts
- Playing at being a storybook character?
- Last in list: shows relative importance

Extract:

There was a cindery path down the garden, ending at a compost heap where eggshells gleamed among leaves and grassclippings. Rags of plastic fluttered from sticks in a bed of cabbages. The girl picked her way daintily, her toes wincing against the cinders. A place in the country. One day she would have a place in the country, but not like this. Sometime. A little white house peeping over a hill, with a stream at the bottom of a crisp green lawn and an orchard with old apple trees and a brown pony. And she would walk in the long grass in this orchard in a straw hat with these two children, a boy and a girl, children with fair shiny hair like hers, and there'd be this man.

Annotations (right):

- Useful – keeps snails and slugs away
- Manmade: signs of warning off or protecting
- Romantic *cliché*
- Further evidence of ideal daydream
- Ideal family; huge self-satisfaction/narcissism
- Sandra clones; repetition. Undefined compared to the house, stream, pony, etc.

1 Use a copy of the extract to add some of your own comments to these annotations.

2 Working with a partner, note down the details given about the inside of Nether Cottage – the objects, the flooring, the smells.

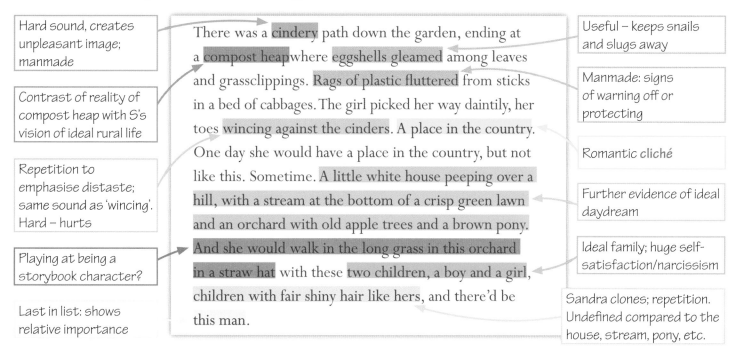

an orchard with old apple trees and a brown pony.

Learning checkpoint

Penelope Lively provides many details of the inside of Nether Cottage: the floor, the clutter, the smells of cabbage, damp and mice. There are also descriptions of ornaments and the biscuit tin.

1 Write brief notes for the following questions:

a Why do you think Lively has included details of all of these things?

b How does Sandra react to them?

c What do the details imply about Mrs Rutter?

d In what ways do they foreshadow the climax of the story?

GETTING IT INTO WRITING

As you have worked through this unit you have been building on your basic understanding of the story by analysing and interpreting the text. The next step is to develop your ideas and practise putting these together into a written response.

1 Use your ideas and notes from this unit to write a response to the following question:

> How do writers present differences between old and young characters in 'The Darkness Out There' and in one other story from *Telling Tales*?
>
> Write about:
>
> • some of the differences that are presented in the two stories
>
> • how the writers present these differences by the ways they write.

Complete this assignment on Cambridge Elevate.

big-eyed flop-eared rabbits and beribboned kittens and flowery milk-maids and a pair of naked chubby children wearing daisy chains.

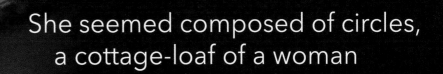

She seemed composed of circles, a cottage-loaf of a woman

Structuring your response

Remember the 'What' and the 'How':

- The 'What' is the 'differences between old and young characters'.
- The 'How' is the writer's way of conveying those differences through language and the use of language devices.

Choosing another story

You should first decide which of the other stories in *Telling Tales* you are going to write about. You have already explored the differences between the father and son in 'Korea', and this might be a good choice.

For the **first** part, you will need to bring together notes you made earlier about the relevant characters (Mrs Rutter; Sandra and Kerry; the father and son in 'Korea'). These will help you to get started. Remember that you are exploring their relationships – how they respond to each other during the course of the stories and how these responses change when something is revealed (the death of the German airman and the idea of fighting for the Unites States).

For the **second** part, you will need to write about the ways in which Lively and McGahern have used language and structure in their stories.

In your response, you could consider the following:

- the importance of language in these two stories, for example the ways in which the physical features of characters are described and how they move
- the ways in which both writers suggest that relationships can change as revelations are made directly (by Mrs Rutter) or overheard (the son)
- the ways in which both writers use settings for their stories, for example the contrasts between inside and outside or the ways in which unpleasant settings are created (Mrs Rutter's cottage or the outside lavatory)
- the ways in which the stories are told ('The Darkness Out There' being a third-person narrative in which the reader is also given Sandra's thoughts and feelings and 'Korea' being a **first-person narrative** with a second narrative by a different character).

Improving your response

1 Here are some extracts from students' responses to the question about old and young characters. Work with a partner to decide which extracts have gone beyond simple comments about the story to a convincing exploration of language or ideas.

2 Choose two of the responses and expand them to explore the differences between old and young characters in 'Korea'.

Student A

Lively presents Mrs Rutter not as an evil character in a fairy story but as an all too credible woman who once had to endure the loss of her young husband who was killed in the war. She claims that she has 'got a sympathy with young people' but in fact this is far from the case. She patronises Kerry and makes inappropriate sexual remarks to Sandra. Whilst perhaps the reader might be able to understand her motive in leaving the German airman to die, the reasons provided, the weather and the puncture, serve to highlight the horror of what she did as does the fact that the airman was calling for his mother, something which Mrs Rutter does not understand. The 'chasm' is not between Sandra and Kerry but between the old and the young.

Student B

Mrs Rutter seems at first to be a pleasant old woman with 'a creamy smiling pool of a face'. When she tells the story about the German airman and how she and her sister left him to die Kerry storms out of her cottage. Sandra follows him. Kerry calls her 'that old bitch' because he thinks that leaving a German airman to die was evil, even though there was a war going on.

Student C

Penelope Lively at first creates a stereotypical old woman. Pat Hammond says that she is 'a dear old thing' and she looks like everyone's ideal granny. Lively describes her as being 'a cottage-loaf of a woman'. Furthermore, Mrs Rutter and Sandra share interests, for example sewing, and both of them look down on Kerry Stevens. Mrs Rutter patronises him with 'I expect that's good steady money if you'd nothing special in mind' and Sandra sneers at his dirty fingernails. However, the tension in the story is not between genders but between ages. What is right for one seems appalling to the other.

Student D

Mrs Rutter is an old woman who lives on her own in a little cottage at the edge of a wood. Sandra and Kerry go to visit her. Kerry mows the grass and Sandra does some dusting. Then Mrs Rutter tells them a story that upsets them both.

Student E

There is a very great gulf between Mrs Rutter and the two young people who visit her. Pat, the organiser of the Good Neighbours' Club, calls Mrs Rutter 'a dear old thing' and makes the reader feel sorry for her because she has 'a wonky leg after her op'. In fact Mrs Rutter is an evil woman, like the witches that Sandra was frightened of when she was younger. At the end of the story Sandra and Kerry start to realise that evil is in other people and not in stories about woods. Mrs Rutter is much scarier than the wolves or even the rapists of Sandra's young imagination.

Student F

Mrs Rutter may seem to be a nice old dear. Pat Hammond thought that she was. In fact it turned out that she and her sister Dot had left a German airman to die slowly after his plane crashed. Both young people are disgusted by this and walk out of her house. Kerry goes first. He may look unappealing but his heart is certainly in the right place. He calls her a 'bitch' and says that 'It makes you want to throw up'. There is obviously a huge difference here between old and young people. The young people have a set of values about right and wrong. Mrs Rutter doesn't.

3 Having thought about these extracts, go back to your own response. What could you do to improve it?

GETTING FURTHER

1 Working with a partner, script or improvise an edition of the TV programme *Through the Keyhole* that visits Nether Cottage.

2 In a small group decide on six questions you would like to ask Penelope Lively about 'The Darkness Out There'.

   a   Swap your questions with another group.
   b   Answer the six questions you've been given as if you were Penelope Lively.

3 One of the lines in a famous rock song is 'I hope I die before I get old'. With advances in medicine, more and more people will live long lives. It has been predicted that one in three children born today will live to be 100 years old.

   a   Is growing old something to be feared or welcomed?
   b   What don't you like about the thought of getting old?
   c   What will be the good things about it?

> She walked behind him, through a world grown unreliable, in which flowers sparkle and birds sing but everything is not as it appears, oh no.

Preparing for your exam

What the exam requires

For your GCSE in English Literature, you will be assessed on *Telling Tales* in **Section A** of **Paper 2: Modern texts and poetry**. The paper lasts for 2 hours and 15 minutes and is worth 60% of your GCSE in English Literature. You have just over **40 minutes** for your answer on *Telling Tales*.

There will be a choice of **two** questions on *Telling Tales*. You must answer **one** of these questions. You will be required to write in detail about **two** different stories from *Telling Tales*. One of the stories will be named in the question. You can choose the other story.

Your answer on *Telling Tales* will be marked out of 30. There will be 4 extra marks available for the accuracy of your writing. **Section B**, on two of the poems you have studied in the Anthology, will be marked out of 30 and **Section C**, on the two unseen poems, will be marked out of 32.

The assessment objective skills

For this question, your answers will be assessed against four assessment objectives (AOs) – skills that you are expected to show. These are outlined below in relationship to your answers. Notice the marks for each assessment objective and take account of this as you manage your time and focus your answer.

- **AO1:** To read, understand and write about what happens in the two stories, referring to the texts and using relevant quotations (12 marks).
- **AO2:** To analyse the language, form and structure used by the two writers to create meanings and effects (12 marks).
- **AO3:** To show an understanding of the context of the stories. This might include, depending on the question, when a particular story was written, the period in which a story was set and why it was set then, its relevance to you in the 21st century (6 marks).
- **AO4:** To use a range of vocabulary and sentence structures for clarity, purpose and effect, with accurate spelling and punctuation (4 marks).

Planning and responding to a question

It is important to spend some minutes at the beginning of the exam:

- choosing the question you want to answer
- making a sensible choice of the second story you will write about
- looking very carefully at the question to make sure you understand exactly what you are being asked to do
- planning what you will write.

Read the following practice question.

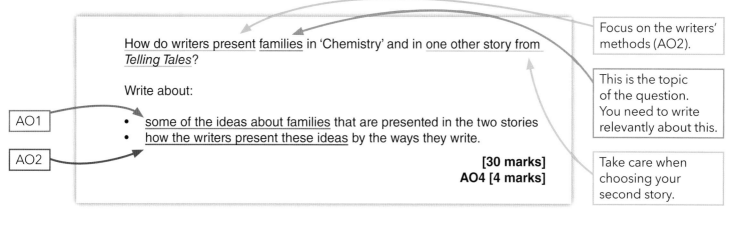

How do writers present <u>families</u> in 'Chemistry' and in <u>one other story</u> from *Telling Tales*?

Write about:

- <u>some of the ideas about families</u> that are presented in the two stories
- <u>how the writers present these ideas</u> by the ways they write.

[30 marks]
AO4 [4 marks]

AO1

AO2

Focus on the writers' methods (AO2).

This is the topic of the question. You need to write relevantly about this.

Take care when choosing your second story.

Planning your answer

One student planned their answer to this question in the following way:

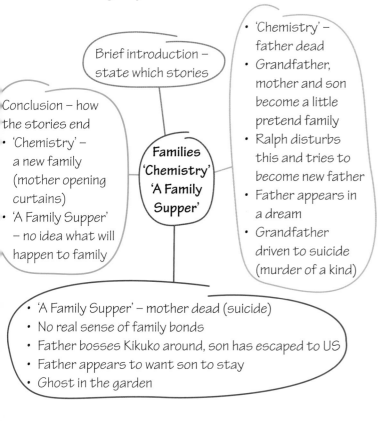

Brief introduction – state which stories

Families 'Chemistry' 'A Family Supper'

- 'Chemistry' – father dead
- Grandfather, mother and son become a little pretend family
- Ralph disturbs this and tries to become new father
- Father appears in a dream
- Grandfather driven to suicide (murder of a kind)

Conclusion – how the stories end
- 'Chemistry' – a new family (mother opening curtains)
- 'A Family Supper' – no idea what will happen to family

- 'A Family Supper' – mother dead (suicide)
- No real sense of family bonds
- Father bosses Kikuko around, son has escaped to US
- Father appears to want son to stay
- Ghost in the garden

Remember:

- The **best answers** will explore the two writers' craft and purposes in creating characters and relationships. They will connect these to the writers' ideas and to the effects upon a reader. They will offer a personal response and many well-explained details.
- **Good answers** will show a clear understanding of how the two writers develop the characters and their relationships, using well-chosen examples.
- **Weaker answers** will only explain what happens to characters and the relationship between them, without using many examples or mentioning how the writers present them.

You must also remember that the two stories you write about must both be relevant to the question on the exam paper you have chosen to answer. In other words, you do need to make **at least one link** between them. **You do not have to compare them throughout your answer** although you can if you want to. However, **no marks are awarded for comparison** on this part of the exam.

'CHEMISTRY' – GRAHAM SWIFT

1 Imagine that you have decided to answer the question below in your exam. Write the first two paragraphs of your answer.

> How do writers present families in 'Chemistry' and in one other story from *Telling Tales*?
>
> Write about:
>
> * some of the ideas about families that are presented in the two stories
> * how the writers present these ideas by the ways they write.
>
> **[30 marks]**
> **AO4 [4 marks]**

✓ **Complete this assignment on Cambridge Elevate.**

To help you think about your own writing, look at these extracts from three students who have answered this question. The annotations show the range of skills displayed in each paragraph. As you read the extracts and the annotations, think how far each example – and your own answer – is successful in:

* using supporting details from the text
* using details to build up an interpretation of the theme of families
* exploring Swift's use of language and structure, as well as his intentions in writing the text.

Student A

This is taken from the opening of Student A's answer:

'Chemistry' begins by showing the reader a sad family. It consists of the grandfather (whose wife has died), the mother (whose husband has died) and the boy whom they look after and who is the narrator of the story. The narrator uses the motor launch as a symbol of the family: the grandfather and boy are united by the line the motor launch sails between them across the pond and the mother looks on. He describes their family as living 'quietly, calmly, even contentedly within the scope of this sad symmetry'. It is a symmetry because it has one person from three generations and it is sad because they have all lost someone they loved. It may be a sad family but it appears to work – until the arrival of Ralph.

Annotations:
- Understands initial part of the story
- Aware of narrative features
- Shows understanding of linguistic features
- An argued interpretation focused on author, contexts and ideas
- Explains the quotation
- Sustains the explanation
- Aware of structural features

In the first paragraph Student A has shown the following skills and achievements:

* a good level of understanding of what happens in the story
* use of one direct quotation with a sustained comment on it
* use of several direct references to the text's narrative, linguistic and structural features
* an answer that is always linked to the question.

2 Working in pairs, decide what advice would you give to Student A on how they could improve their answer.

Student B

This is taken from Student B's answer:

The family house, where Grandfather and his wife Vera had spent almost all of their married life, soon becomes a battleground with Ralph as the invading force. Swift implies that Ralph wants to become a second father to the boy when he offers to buy him a new motor launch. The boy says "No!', several times, fiercely.' Swift emphasises the boy's dislike of Ralph by writing that the 'No!' was repeated and that it was said 'fiercely' to show the boy's defiance. The implication is clearly that in rejecting the present, the boy is also rejecting Ralph as a father figure. The boy wishes the family to continue as it was, a quiet, sad, self-contained unit.

Begins to offer an interpretation; close link to question
Further interpretation
Relevant, well-selected quotation
Interpretation of quotation
Secure understanding of Swift's characterisation
Interpretation of the story up to this point

This is a stronger answer than Student A's. In this part of the answer, Student B is clearly focused on the author's craft. The answer engages with Swift's use of language and characterisation and develops interpretations about the family. It shows:

* understanding of Swift's characterisation
* sustained comment on meaning of textual detail
* a developed consideration of the boy and his wishes for his family.

3 Working in pairs, decide what advice would you give to Student B on how they could improve their answer.

Student C

This is taken from Student C's answer:

Swift presents the change in the family unit as being almost animalistic: the old leader is ousted, and, as the boy believes, murdered, by the young leader. Ralph's assertiveness does not just dominate the mother, he wears her husband's old sweater 'which was far too small for him'. Physically and emotionally he has dominated the mother. The boy sees her 'go soft and heavy and blurred' when she drinks, indicating that she becomes less of a woman and more of a possession of Ralph. He, in contrast, gains in authority, the alcohol fuelling his masculinity and implying his new dominance of the family. At the end, the mother clears away all evidence of the grandfather, declaring the start of a new family – 'There, isn't that lovely?'. Swift leaves the reader in no doubt that the new order will be a very long way from 'lovely'.

4 This is the best of the three answers. Working in pairs, annotate the answer to show what Student C has achieved. What evidence can you find that this is a convincing analysis that shows careful thought and consideration of several aspects of the story, the writer's craft and intentions?

'ODOUR OF CHRYSANTHEMUMS' – D.H. LAWRENCE

1 Read the following practice question on 'Odour of Chrysanthemums':

> How do writers present the settings of their stories in 'Odour of Chrysanthemums' and in one other story from *Telling Tales*?
>
> Write about:
>
> - some of the ideas about families that are presented in the two stories
> - how the writers present these ideas by the ways they write.
>
> **[30 marks]**
> **AO4 [4 marks]**

Complete this assignment on Cambridge Elevate.

To answer this question you should think about the area surrounding the cottage, what the outside of the cottage looks like and what is inside the cottage. Write three paragraphs in answer to the question.

2 Working in pairs, decide which of the following annotations you feel belongs with which of the following student extracts:

1 Simple comments, which show the student has read and understood the story and are relevant to the question asked. Might identify one or two aspects of the language or structure and a main theme.

2 Structured comments that are explained and make a range of relevant points and show some understanding of themes.

3 A clear understanding of the story and its language, structure and themes, which is sustained throughout the answer and uses references to the text well.

4 Relevant comments supported by some references to the text. Might identify some of the effects on the reader of the language or structure. Shows some awareness of themes.

5 A convincing analysis that shows careful thought and consideration of several aspects of the story, the writer's craft and intentions.

6 A thoughtful consideration, which is developed because it explores several characters, features or themes in detail and may offer alternative interpretations.

Student A

The cottage where Elizabeth and her children live is depressing. Outside there is a yard and a garden with a few flowers and trees. There are also some cabbages, which are 'ragged' so you wouldn't want to eat them. Even the pink chrysanthemums are sickly.

Student B

Lawrence shows the poverty of the Bates's household in his description of the cottage. It is 'low' and he describes it as 'squatting' as though it were a small animal. He also writes that a vine 'clutched at the house' making it seem as if it is threatened.

Student C

Lawrence creates a meagre, impoverished setting for the events in the story. The outside world is 'withered' and dusk is personified as having 'crept' into the spinney. The Bates's cottage is 'clutched' by a vine 'as if to claw down the tiled roof'. The use of the verb 'clawing' gives the vine animalistic qualities: the vine is trying to destroy the house as one animal might claw another. The lives of the people who live there, by implication, are also being clawed. The detailed description creates an atmosphere of dereliction and threat.

Student D

The setting of the story is depressing. Everything by the railway line is dead and there are rats in the yard outside Elizabeth's cottage. The only nice thing in the story is her fire, which gives the cottage warmth.

Student E

Twice in his creation of the setting Lawrence mentions the pink chrysanthemums. The first time they are 'dishevelled' and compared to 'pink cloths'. Like everything else in the immediate area they are pitiful things, objects that can be 'hung' rather than growing naturally. The second mention is when John tears at the 'ragged wisps', again emphasising their diseased nature. When John scatters the petals along the path, Lawrence uses his action as a mockery of strewing petals before a bridal procession or the crowning of a May Queen. To his mother they look 'nasty' but she cannot help but try to find a sort of beauty in them for she breaks of a twig and holds it against her face, perhaps in a memory of her marriage.

Student F

The area around the cottage is 'forsaken', 'dreary' and even the light is 'stagnant'. The area is dominated by the pit with the red flames. This makes everything else seem small in comparison by emphasising how important the pit is and how nobody can escape it.

'MY POLISH TEACHER'S TIE' – HELEN DUNMORE

Here are two questions on 'My Polish Teacher's Tie' that might be asked in a GCSE English Literature exam.

How do writers present relationships in 'My Polish Teacher's Tie' and in one other story from *Telling Tales*?

Write about:

- some of the ideas about relationships that are presented in the two stories
- how the writers present these ideas by the ways they write.

[30 marks]
AO4 [4 marks]

✓ Complete this assignment on Cambridge Elevate.

How do writers use symbols in 'My Polish Teacher's Tie' and in one other story from *Telling Tales*?

Write about:

- the meaning of the symbols
- how the writers present the symbols by the ways they write.

[30 marks]
AO4 [4 marks]

---

1 Discuss what each of Students A–F has achieved and what they might need to do to improve their answer.

Student A

Steve's poem to Carla is about a bird in a coal mine. The bird fell down the mine and sang to call for help. No help came and the bird died. The bird is like Carla. Steve thinks she is singing for help to find who she really is. But she doesn't have to die because he finds her.

Student B

There are many unequal relationships in the story. For example Dunmore makes it quite plain that there is a hierarchy within the school and that Carla is at the bottom. She does this by making the Head struggle to remember her name, 'Oh, er – Mrs, er – Carter'. The repetition of 'er' and the dashes indicate that he can scarcely remember her name. Her only importance to him is as a provider of tea and buns: she is completely without individuality in his eyes and serves only a menial function in his school. Carla, on the other hand, does not have a high opinion of him. Dunmore shows this in 'He stitched a nice smile on his face', the implication being that nice smiles are part of his professional repertoire and do not come easily to him.

Student C

In a way the stale buns become a symbol of Valerie Kenward's selfishness. While she always complains that she is on a diet, she always takes 'the biggest bun'. She likes to imagine that she is a very important person, perhaps because she is a teacher, and her importance is measured by the size of her buns. On the day of Steve's arrival, the buns are stale but she still takes one, while complaining about the cost.

Student D

Dunmore uses the phrase 'a terribly hopeful tie'. This is may be to differentiate Steve from the rest of the teachers in the staffroom or to emphasise his naivety and childlike qualities or it may be to show that it is possible for people to overcome artificial barriers of geography and social class and join together to celebrate what they have in common – in this case their Polish roots, or ties. Dunmore compares the tie to 'a flag from another country' adding 'a better country than the ones either of us lived in'. Thus it becomes a 'hopeful' symbol of a future in which people can celebrate who they really are.

Student E

Valerie Kenward and Carla Carter seem to have very different relationships with their daughters. Valerie seems to indulge her daughter and spoil her. Carla is very sarcastic, saying, 'If ever anyone brought up their kids to be pleased with themselves it's Valerie Kenward' which means that Philippa is very stuck up and arrogant. She even laughs at Steve's accent. Carla seems to be kind to her daughter Jade. Carla drives Jade to her friend's house and gives her a poetry book. This is a much more loving and kinder relationship.

Student F

Carla likes Steve very much and she enjoys his letters and poems. When he is going to visit her school she feels very worried because she thinks he will not want to meet a dinner lady. She plucks up the courage to introduce herself to him and he is surprised and then really pleased. He holds her hands and sings to her. This is a surprising thing to do in a school staffroom and shows how happy he is to see her.

2 Now, on your own, try to answer one of the questions on 'My Polish Teacher's Tie'.

3 Once you have written your response, ask your partner to suggest ways in which you could improve your answer.

'KOREA' – JOHN MCGAHERN

Imagine that you have decided to answer the question below in your exam.

> How do writers present unexpected events and their consequences in 'Korea' and in one other story from *Telling Tales*?
>
> Write about:
>
> - some of the ideas about the unexpected events and their consequences that are presented in the two stories
> - how the writers present these ideas by the ways they write.
>
> [30 marks]
> AO4 [4 marks]

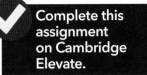

Complete this assignment on Cambridge Elevate.

1 First plan and then write three paragraphs of your own to answer this question. Each paragraph should be on a different unexpected event and its consequences.

Now read the following paragraphs by three students who have answered this question.

Student A

This is taken from the opening of Student A's answer:

An example of an unexpected event comes at the start of the story. The father has spoken of his time in prison in Mountjoy and the execution he watched. Two men were chosen in <u>what seems to have been a random way to be executed as a reprisal or revenge for the deaths of the British soldiers</u>. The father clearly remembers the young man whose <u>buttons flew into the air</u> when he had been shot and before he fell to the ground. The consequence was that years later, when he is on his honeymoon, the father is reminded of the buttons by <u>the furze pods bursting in all directions</u>. He says that '<u>It destroyed the day</u>'. This seems to mean that <u>he did not enjoy his honeymoon</u> and that the <u>memory of the execution has stayed with him</u>. It is strange that he was so affected by the execution and yet he can consider the death of his own son in Korea.

| Clear understanding of story and context |
| Close reference to the text |
| Good concentration on the exam question asked |
| A second close reference to the text |
| Relevant direct quotation |
| Comment on quotation |
| Sustained comment on quotation |

Student A has shown:

- a good level of understanding of what happens in the story
- use of one direct quotation with a sustained comment on it
- use of several direct references to the text's narrative, linguistic and structural features
- an answer that is always linked to the question.

2 Working in pairs, decide what advice you would give to Student A on how they could improve their answer.

Student B

This is taken from Student B's answer:

The death of Luke Moran was obviously completely unexpected but has two important consequences. The first is the way in which his life was given an importance by his death: in the small world of rural Ireland his corpse is given a considerable amount of military dignity. 'Shots had been fired above the grave'. This is in direct contrast to the shots that were fired at Mountjoy. Luke was celebrated as being a hero with a flag 'draped' over his 'leaden casket' and 'decorations' presented by 'a military attaché', all of which McGahern implies impressed the local people and elevated Luke's status by his seemingly heroic death. The second consequence is that his father was paid ten thousand dollars and is able to buy cattle 'left and right', making himself a rich man. The death of the son has led to his father acquiring unexpected wealth and enjoying using it.

Annotations:
- Understands context of story
- Interpretation of narrative
- Understands McGahern's intentions
- A succession of well-selected, relevant quotations
- Interpretation of quotations
- Begins to explore – death might not have been heroic
- Develops the answer to cover the second consequence
- Interpretation of characterisation

This is a stronger answer than Student A's. It shows:

- understanding of McGahern's characterisation
- sustained comment on meaning of textual detail
- a thoughtful and developed consideration of both the event and its two separate consequences.

3 Working in pairs, decide what advice would you give to Student B on how they could improve their answer.

Student C

This is taken from Student C's answer:

'I knew my youth had ended' – McGahern locates the narrator in an outside lavatory, 'in the smell of shit and piss', creating a setting as unpleasant as the unexpected conversation he overhears. The language is monosyllabic and shocking. The message is clear: the narrator is degraded and dehumanised. Every bond between father and son has been broken as the realisation dawns that his father is prepared to treat him as a commodity to be sold, ideally as a corpse, a piece of dead meat with a large price tag which would allow him to retire from fishing and live a life of some comfort. The paucity of the setting with the warm smell of the worms and the inadequate amount of clay stands as a contrast to the life his father could have if, ironically, his son was fortunate enough to be killed. His son and the young solider executed at Mountjoy are coupled in a sense of needless, premature death. The father and son are also ironically linked - 'as if I too had to prepare myself to murder'. It is a consequence that can never be altered.

4 This is the best of the three answers. Working in pairs, annotate the answer to show what Student C has achieved. What evidence can you find that this is a convincing analysis that shows careful thought and consideration of several aspects of the story, the writer's craft and intentions?

'A FAMILY SUPPER' – KAZUO ISHIGURO

Read the following practice exam question:

> How do writers present fathers and their relationships with their children in 'A Family Supper' and in one other story from *Telling Tales*?
>
> Write about:
>
> - some of the ideas about fathers and their relationships with their children that are presented in the two stories
> - how the writers present these ideas by the ways they write.
>
> [30 marks]
> AO4 [4 marks]

✓ Complete this assignment on Cambridge Elevate.

Student A decided to write about 'Korea' as well as 'A Family Supper' and planned their answer like this:

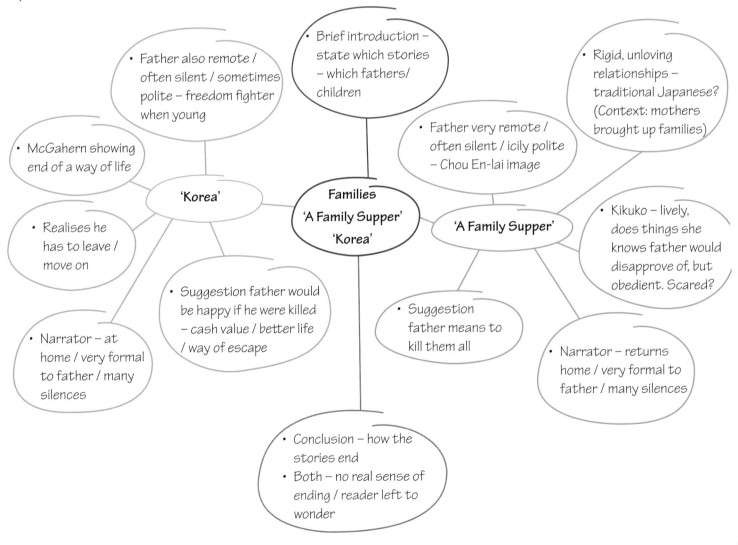

- Father also remote / often silent / sometimes polite – freedom fighter when young
- Brief introduction – state which stories – which fathers/children
- Rigid, unloving relationships – traditional Japanese? (Context: mothers brought up families)
- McGahern showing end of a way of life
- Father very remote / often silent / icily polite – Chou En-lai image
- 'Korea'
- Families 'A Family Supper' 'Korea'
- 'A Family Supper'
- Realises he has to leave / move on
- Kikuko – lively, does things she knows father would disapprove of, but obedient. Scared?
- Narrator – at home / very formal to father / many silences
- Suggestion father would be happy if he were killed – cash value / better life / way of escape
- Suggestion father means to kill them all
- Narrator – returns home / very formal to father / many silences
- Conclusion – how the stories end
- Both – no real sense of ending / reader left to wonder

Student A then wrote five paragraphs about 'A Family Supper':

The father in 'A Family Supper' seems to be a very remote figure. We learn that his wife had died two years before his son returned home from America but he had not bothered to tell him how his mother had died. He seems a very strict man and looks like Chou En-lai, the Chinese Premier. He does not speak a lot and the story has many moments of silence. He has his own special room where he makes plastic models of battleships. He thinks that Mr Watanabe was a good man because he committed suicide when their joint business went bankrupt. The father, on the other hand, did not commit suicide.

His daughter seems to be afraid of him and hides what she is doing and her plans for the future from him. She has a boyfriend and she smokes. These are both things he would disapprove of. She also hitch-hikes. She even has plans to go to America, depending on her relationship with her boyfriend. Her father appears to treat her like a servant. He leaves her to cook since it is a skill he is not proud of but he does say that she is a good girl. At the end of the story he sends her out to make the tea.

The father's relationship with his son seems to be very cold and formal. When the boy was young his father hit him around the head for talking too much. Something bad had happened before the narrator left for America because the father says that he is prepared to forget the past but we never get to discover exactly what had happened. The father blames other people for the narrator's behaviour and says that he did not know what he was doing. The father is upset when the narrator does not recognise a photo of his mother.

It is important that the narrator does not recognise his own mother because in Japanese families it is the mother who brings the children up. Fathers tend to be much more remote. That is one of the reasons both children seem to feel sorrow for their mother's death. Their father offers them no comfort and even serves them fish for their supper, knowing that it would remind them both of their dead mother. It is not clear whether the mother ate the fugu on purpose to kill herself or whether it was just that she did not want to be impolite to her school friend.

The fish supper may mean that the father is trying to kill his whole family. We are never sure what sort of fish it is and the father even offers his son the last piece. He may be planning what he considers to be an honourable suicide like Mr Watanabe's. Whether he really means this or not, his relationship with his children is hard and cold and there is no love in the house.

1 Working in pairs, look at each paragraph in turn and improve it. You could do this by adding to it or by completely rewriting the paragraphs or using some or all of the ideas each one contains.

You should think about:

- using direct quotations from the text
- exploring Ishiguro's characterisation in more depth, especially of the father
- analysing Ishiguro's use of language, structure and narrative voice
- exploring Ishiguro's intentions in writing the story.

'INVISIBLE MASS OF THE BACK ROW' – CLAUDETTE WILLIAMS

Here are two questions on 'Invisible Mass of the Back Row' that might be asked in a GCSE English Literature exam:

> How do writers present adults in 'Invisible Mass of the Back Row' and in one other story from *Telling Tales*?
>
> Write about:
>
> - some of the ideas about adults that are presented in the two stories
> - how the writers present these ideas by the ways they write.
>
> **[30 marks]**
> **AO4 [4 marks]**

✓ **Complete this assignment on Cambridge Elevate.**

> How do writers present young people in 'Invisible Mass of the Back Row' and in one other story from *Telling Tales*?
>
> Write about:
>
> - some of the ideas about young people that are presented in the two stories
> - how the writers present these ideas by the ways they write.
>
> **[30 marks]**
> **AO4 [4 marks]**

Student A decided to write on the first question, using 'My Polish Teacher's Tie' as their second text. This is their plan:

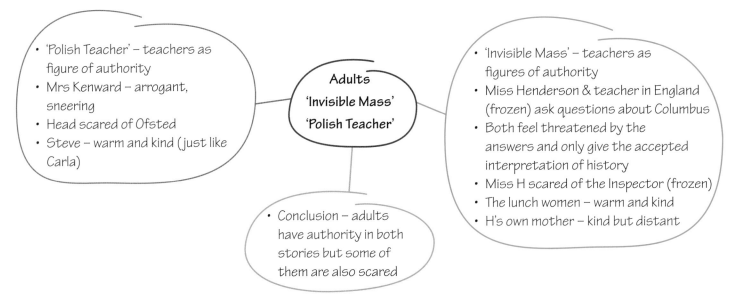

- 'Polish Teacher' – teachers as figure of authority
- Mrs Kenward – arrogant, sneering
- Head scared of Ofsted
- Steve – warm and kind (just like Carla)

Adults
'Invisible Mass'
'Polish Teacher'

- 'Invisible Mass' – teachers as figures of authority
- Miss Henderson & teacher in England (frozen) ask questions about Columbus
- Both feel threatened by the answers and only give the accepted interpretation of history
- Miss H scared of the Inspector (frozen)
- The lunch women – warm and kind
- H's own mother – kind but distant

- Conclusion – adults have authority in both stories but some of them are also scared

This is the opening of Student A's answer:

Many of the adults in 'Invisible Mass of the Back Row' are cold, authoritarian figures who see their job as imparting one particular version of history – Columbus's 'conquest' of the Caribbean. Both the Inspector and the teacher in England have faces that Williams describes as being 'frozen', showing both their lack of warmth for their students and their anger at being challenged. 'Frozen' indicates a lack of human feeling: these teachers are little better than automata. Williams writes about the students' 'imprisonment' and calls the teachers 'jailers' whose job is to maintain order in the classroom and order in society as a whole. As Hortense's uncle says, it is an exercise in group humiliation against 'All de poor black people dem'.

Student B decided to write on the second question, using 'The Darkness Out There' as their second text. This is their plan:

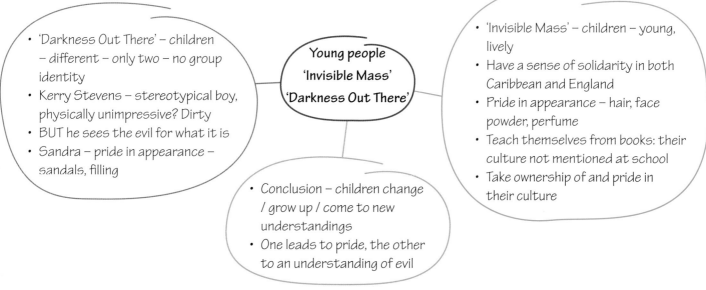

- 'Darkness Out There' – children – different – only two – no group identity
- Kerry Stevens – stereotypical boy, physically unimpressive? Dirty
- BUT he sees the evil for what it is
- Sandra – pride in appearance – sandals, filling

Young people
'Invisible Mass'
'Darkness Out There'

- 'Invisible Mass' – children – young, lively
- Have a sense of solidarity in both Caribbean and England
- Pride in appearance – hair, face powder, perfume
- Teach themselves from books: their culture not mentioned at school
- Take ownership of and pride in their culture

- Conclusion – children change / grow up / come to new understandings
- One leads to pride, the other to an understanding of evil

This is the opening of Student B's answer:

Williams creates a sense of solidarity between the girls who sit on the back row because they are not bright. After Hortense has moved to England, she remains on the back row. Williams is implying that the experience of school is universal: some girls always end up on the back row; others, like Lorna Phillips, sit at the front being brighter, prettier and richer. Williams shows that discrimination can come in many forms in the school environment and must be challenged and exposed. For her it is the solidarity of students that is important as they form a mutually supportive group of individuals who together form the Back Row team. For Hortense, school has to be endured rather than enjoyed. Williams describes it as a 'rank, smelly room' and 'the steam bath', the sense of heat creating a feeling of discomfort, especially as the classroom holds 50 students.

1 Choose one of the two answers and, using the relevant plan above, continue to write it.

'THE DARKNESS OUT THERE' – PENELOPE LIVELY

Imagine that you have decided to answer the question below in your exam.

> How do writers present characters whose beliefs are challenged in some way in 'The Darkness Out There' and in one other story from *Telling Tales*?
>
> Write about:
>
> - some of the ideas about loss of innocence that are presented in the two stories
> - how the writers present these ideas by the ways they write.
>
> **[30 marks]**
> **AO4 [4 marks]**

✔ Complete this assignment on Cambridge Elevate.

1 First decide which other story to use, then plan and then write your own answer to this question.

Now read the following paragraphs by three students who have answered this question.

Student A

This is taken from the opening of Student A's answer:

At the start of the story Sandra is a very naive young girl. She believes that people are exactly what they seem, preferring Mrs Carpenter at the King's Arms over Pat because Mrs Carpenter wears heeled boots and Pat has a squint. This makes Sandra wonder 'Are people who help other people always not very nice-looking?' . Sandra herself takes a great pride in her own appearance and admires her feet. She is worried about having a tiny filling. When she first meets Mrs Rutter she is fooled by Mrs Rutter's appearance. She does not notice her glittering eyes and thinks she is a harmless 'cottage-loaf of a woman'. It is only after the story of the airman and Kerry's appalled reaction to it that she comes to realise just what sort of person Mrs Rutter really is.

Annotations:
- A number of close references to the text
- A well-selected direct quotation but there is no direct comment on it
- Clear understanding of character
- Further close reference to the text
- Further understanding of character
- A well-selected direct quotation but again no comment on it
- Clear understanding of story

Student A has shown:

- a good level of understanding of what happens in the story
- use of two direct quotations but without any comments on these
- use of several direct references to the text's narrative, linguistic and structural features
- a clear understanding of Sandra's character
- an answer that is always linked to the question.

2 Working in pairs, improve Student A's answer by adding four new sentences.

Student B

This is taken from Student B's answer:

Penelope Lively shows <u>a rather immature, self-satisfied young girl</u> suddenly exposed to real cruelty. For her, <u>Packer's End holds fear because of what she has been told</u>. When she was little she thought it was a place of fairytale evil, of '<u>witches and wolves</u>', <u>the alliteration adding to the storybook nature of the fear</u>. As she grew up she became scared of the rumours of men with knives, 'two enormous blokes, sort of gypsy types', <u>but Lively makes it clear that this is not a fear to be taken seriously when she writes 'sort of'</u>. Lively shows the fear as being groundless as it is based on rumour '<u>people at school said</u>' and ill-defined. <u>Only later does Sandra meet the real thing</u> and <u>it shocks her to her core as the world has 'grown unreliable'. Her beliefs are shattered and it seems that she will have great difficulty in coming to terms with what she has experienced.</u>

Interpretation of characterisation
Understands context
Well-selected quotation
Comment on language and effect
Comment on effect of language
Well-selected quotation
Clear understanding of narrative structure
Clear understanding of characterisation supported by well-selected quotation

This is a stronger answer than Student A's. It engages with Lively's use of language and characterisation and begins to develop ideas about Sandra's loss of innocence. It shows:

- understanding of Lively's characterisation
- sustained comment on meaning of textual detail
- a thoughtful and developed consideration of Lively's initial characterisation of Sandra and the way in which this changes.

3 Working in pairs, improve Student B's answer by adding six new sentences.

Student C

This is taken from Student C's answer:

Lively provides Sandra with an indistinct belief in her future happiness: her partner will be 'this man', undefined and indistinct. Lively gives Sandra an innocent, naive self-image. Sandra is full of childish beliefs about her own image and her future. She thinks only in terms of romantic clichés. She admires her own body and realises that she is physically maturing. This new maturity does not seem to be accompanied by a maturing of her aspirations. These are limited by travel brochures and fairy tale images of a little white house 'peeping over a hill'. Lively's use of 'peeping' makes the house seem both infantile and cut off from the world. The succession of details, the stream, the lawn, the apple trees and the pony emphasise the innocence of her beliefs. At other times, Lively provides other, more concrete, aspirations: Sandra is a girl who believes in the value of a sewing machine.

4 This is the best of the three answers. Working in pairs, annotate the answer to show what Student C has achieved. What evidence can you find that this is a convincing analysis that shows careful thought and consideration of several aspects of the story, the writer's craft and intentions?

THEMES AND IDEAS

A group of students was asked to make links between the themes and ideas of the short stories. Their findings are in the following table:

Themes and ideas	'Chemistry'	'Odour of Chrysanthemums'	'My Polish Teacher's Tie'	'Korea'	'A Family Supper'	'Invisible Mass of the Back Row'	'The Darkness Out There'
Identity			✔		✔	✔	
Death	✔	✔		✔	✔		✔
Power	✔			✔		✔	
Loneliness	✔	✔			✔		
Honour				✔	✔	✔	
Grief	✔	✔			✔		
Society			✔	✔		✔	
Parents and children	✔	✔	✔	✔	✔	✔	
Adults and children	✔	✔	✔	✔	✔	✔	✔
The past and the present	✔			✔	✔		✔
Voice	✔	✔	✔	✔	✔	✔	✔
Relationships	✔	✔	✔	✔	✔	✔	✔
Stereotypes			✔		✔	✔	✔
Things not as they seem	✔	✔	✔	✔	✔		✔
Food defines character	✔		✔		✔	✔	✔

 Working in a small group, discuss why ten of these links were made. For each link, try to consider at least three stories.

 Then create some links of your own.

Tip

Finally …

To prepare for your exam, the most important thing is to keep going back to the stories themselves. Student Books, revision guides and the internet can help, but the important thing is to keep reading the stories and thinking, talking and writing about them. You need the stories at your fingertips.

And remember the words of the Goose in *Charlotte's Web*:

Luck has nothing to do with it! It was good management and hard work.

Glossary

annotate to write notes on a text to highlight details

atmosphere the feelings created by a writer's description of a setting

connotation an idea or a feeling linked to the main meaning of a word – what it implies or suggests in addition to its literal meaning

cliché a very overused or unoriginal phrase

context the historical circumstances of a piece of writing, which affect what an author wrote and why they wrote it

dialogue where two or more characters are speaking to each other

first-person narrative an account of events written from a personal point of view (so using 'I' or 'we' rather than 'he', 'she' or 'they')

foreshadow to hint at what lies ahead, often in the sense of a warning

irony the use of words to imply the opposite of, or something different from, what is said

metaphor an imaginative comparison in which one thing is said to be another

omniscient all-seeing and all-knowing. The omniscient narrator of a story knows more than the reader about the situation and how it will develop

pace the speed at which something happens, for example the speed at which a story develops

patois the dialect of people from a particular area or region

pun a 'play on words' – the use of a word with a double meaning. A pun may have the same spelling but different meanings or different spellings (and different meanings) but sound alike

setting the description of the place in which a story is set

simile an imaginative comparison that uses 'like' or 'as'

slang informal language

standard English the variety of English used in public communication

storyboard to make a sequence of drawings that show the different scenes in a story

symbolism the use of one thing to represent another

third-person narrative an account of events using 'he', 'she' or 'they', rather than 'I' or 'we'

viewpoint the position from which a character sees things

Picture credits

cover Walter Bibikow/Getty; p.5 Milosz_G/Thinkstock; p.6 Stage89/Thinkstock; p.10t moodboard/Thinkstock; p.10cl Jeff Morgan 11/Alamy; p.10cr Jemal Countess/Thinkstock; p.10b Jason Merritt/Thinkstock; p.11 GARY DOAK/Alamy; p.12 SerrNovik/Thinkstock; p.14 mm88/Thinkstock; p.16 mikcz/Thinkstock; p.20 RyanKing999/Thinkstock; p.23 DmitriMaruta/Thinkstock; p.24 Jose Luis Pelaez Inc../Thinkstock; p.25t Tombizarre/Thinkstock; p.25br Heritage Image Partnership Ltd/Alamy; p.25bl Heritage Image Partnership Ltd/Alamy; p.25c Heritage Image Partnership Ltd /Alamy; p.26 Pictorial Press Ltd/Alamy; p.27 Roger Worsley Archive/Mary Evans; p.30 altocumulus/Thinkstock; p.32 sodapix sodapix/Thinkstock; p.33 mansum008/Thinkstock; p.34 creepers888/Thinkstock; p.36 Butsaya/Thinkstock; p.37 showcake/Thinkstock; p.38 voraorn/Thinkstock; p.39 Martina_L/Thinkstock; p.40 Geraint Lewis/Alamy; p.41 Fernando Miranda/Thinkstock; p.43 Leighton-Anthony Miller/Thinkstock; p.46 Eric Isselée/Thinkstock; p.48 Nastco/Thinkstock; p.49 alexaldo/Thinkstock; p.51 YuliaBuchatskaya/Thinkstock; p.53t Archive Image/Alamy; p.53b udra/Thinkstock; p.54 Ulf Andersen/Getty; p.56 Charles Iain Colquhoun/Thinkstock; p.58 UrosPoteko/Thinkstock; p.60 Jan Tyler/Thinkstock; p.61 Wavebreakmedia Ltd/Thinkstock; p.63 catolla/Thinkstock; p.64 Cienpies Design/Shutterstock; p.65 Hemera Technologies/Thinkstock; p.67 BLACK STAR FILMS/Kobal; p.68t–b karandaev/Thinkstock; Maroš Markovič/Fotolia; Devon Stephens/Alamy; warayut/Thinkstock; p.69 Geraint Lewis/Alamy; p.71 Anthony Brown/Thinkstock; p.72 Lario Tus/Shutterstock; p.73 Simeon Flowers/Thinkstock; p.75 takayuki/Shutterstock; p.76 nvelichko/Thinkstock; p.79 Geoff du Feu/Alamy; p.81tl WitchEra/Shutterstock; p.81tr inci aral/Thinkstock; p.81c steve & ghy sampson/Getty RF; p.81br Urbanmyth Images/Alamy; p.81bl inci aral/Thinkstock; p.82 imw0160323/Topfoto; p.85 Rohit Seth/Shutterstock; p.86 Nanisimova/Thinkstock; p.89 Joseph Sohm/Shutterstock; p.90 Everett Collection Historical/Alamy; p.91 Lorrie Dallek/Alamy; p.93 Bikeworldtravel/Thinkstock; p.95 Popperfoto/Getty; p.96t Stage89/Thinkstock; p.96b clairevis/Thinkstock; p.96b (background) pialhovik/Thinkstock; p.97 Jeremy Moeran/Alamy; p.98 IakovKalinin/Thinkstock; p.99 Milosz_G/Thinkstock; p.100 PaweÅ Aniszewski/Thinkstock; p.103 Carmelka/Thinkstock; p.105 destillat/Thinkstock; p.106 cjmacer/Shutterstock; p.107 Food and Drink Photos/Alamy; p.109 RobBlair07/Thinkstock; p.110 vectorarts/Thinkstock.

Text credits

The authors and publishers acknowledge the following sources of copyright material and are grateful for the permissions granted. While every effort has been made, it has not always been possible to identify the sources of all the material used, or to trace all copyright holders. If any omissions are brought to our notice, we will be happy to include the appropriate acknowledgements on reprinting.

p.10 *Chemistry: A Volatile History – Discovering the Elements* Episode 1 of 3 BBC Four – 21/01/2010 21:00 and again on BBC Four 21/3/2015 19:00. Presenter Jim Al-Khalili, Executive Producer Sacha Baveystock, Producer/Director Jon Stephens, Production Manager Giselle Corbett; p.11 Guardian News & Media – Susanna Rustin, Saturday 5 July 2014; p.16 Graham Swift: 'Chemistry' from *Learning to Swim and Other Stories*, Panmacmillan; p.40 A P Watt at United Agents on behalf of Helen Dunmore. www.helendunmore.com/about.asp; p.44 Helen Dunmore: 'My Polish Teacher's Tie' from *Ice Cream*, published by Penguin; p.47 Helen Dunmore: 'My Polish Teacher's Tie' from *Ice Cream*, published by Penguin; p.54 Eamon Maher, The Liffey Press; *John McGahern: From the Local to the Universal*, published by The Liffey Press; p.55 John McGahern: 'Korea' from *Creatures of the Earth: New and Selected Short Stories*, published by Faber & Faber; p.61 John McGahern: *All Will Be Well: A Memoir*, published by Alfred A. Knopf; p.62 John McGahern: 'Korea' from *Creatures of the Earth: New and Selected Short Stories*, published by Faber & Faber; p.69 Interview: David Sexton Meets Kazuo Ishiguro – David Sexton 1987 from the London Literary Review (January 1987), pp. 16-19. Reprinted by permission of the London Literary Review; p.75 In Conversation with Kazuo Ishiguro – Christopher Bigsby / 1987 from *Writers in Conversation* Vol 1, pp. 193-204. Reprinted by permission of Pen & Inc Press. - 978-1902913070, Pen & Inc Press (1 Mar. 2001); p.78 An Interview with Kazuo Ishiguro – Gregory Mason / 1986 Gregory Mason / 1986 from *Contemporary Literature*, vol. 30, no. 3 (Autumn 1989). Copyright © 1989. Reprinted by permission of the University of Wisconsin Press; p.78 David Sexton Meets Kazuo Ishiguro – David Sexton 1987 from London Literary Review (January 1987), pp. 16-19. The London Literary Review; p.83 *Charting the Journey*, edited by Shabnam Grewal et al, published by Sheba Feminist Press; p.85 *Charting the Journey*, edited by Shabnam Grewal et al, published by Sheba Feminist Press; p.85 Claudette Williams: 'Invisible Mass of the Back Row' from *Stories of Many Cultures*, published by Hodder and Stoughton; p.87 Claudette Williams: 'Invisible Mass of the Back Row' from *Stories of Many Cultures*, Hodder and Stoughton; p.88 *Charting the Journey*, edited by Shabnam Grewal et al, published by Sheba Feminist Press; p.97 Penelope Lively: *Moon Tiger*, published by Penguin; p.105 Penelope Lively: 'The Darkness Out There' from *Pack of Cards: Stories 1978-1986*, published by Penguin.

Produced for Cambridge University Press by

White-Thomson Publishing
www.wtpub.co.uk

Project editor: Rachel Minay
Designer: Kim Williams, 320 Media
Picture research: Izzi Howell